EXPLORATIONS

STUDIES IN CULTURE AND COMMUNICATION

VOLUME 4

I0027276

Edited by Edmund Carpenter and
Marshall McLuhan

WIPF & STOCK · Eugene, Oregon

Wipf and Stock Publishers
199 W 8th Ave, Suite 3
Eugene, OR 97401

Explorations 4
Studies in Culture and Communication
By Carpenter, E S and Easterbrook, W T
Copyright©1954, Edmund S. Carpenter & Marshall McLuhan Estates
ISBN 13: 978-1-62032-430-1
Publication date 9/28/2016
Previously published by University of Toronto, 1955

This is an anniversary new edition of the eight co-edited issues of Explorations, with annotations by Michael Darroch and Janine Marchessault, in conjunction with students and researchers at the University of Windsor and York University, Canada. Research for the annotated editions was made possible by a grant from the Social Sciences and Humanities Research Council of Canada. Additional research was provided by Lorraine Spiess in conjunction with the Estate of Edmund Carpenter. Permissions research was provided by Jonathan McKenzie. This republication project was a joint initiative undertaken by the estates of Marshall McLuhan and Edmund Carpenter.

Funding for Issues 1–6 (1953–1956) was originally provided by a grant from the Ford Foundation's Behavioral Sciences Program. Issues 7–8 (1957) were sponsored by the Telegram of Toronto.

Typography for Issue 1 was designed and printed by Rous & Mann Press Limited, Toronto. The cover of Issue 7 and the cover and typography of Issue 8 were designed by Harley Parker and printed courtesy of the University of Toronto Press. Please see individual issues for further notes on contributors and acknowledgements.

Every effort has been made to contact copyright holders and to ensure that all the information presented is correct. Some of the facts in this volume may be subject to debate or dispute. If proper copyright acknowledgment has not been made, or for clarifications and corrections, please contact the publishers and we will correct the information in future reprintings, if any.

EXPLORATIONS . . .

is designed, not as a permanent reference journal that embalms truth for posterity, but as a publication that explores and searches and questions.

We envisage a series that will cut across the humanities and social sciences by treating them as a continuum. We believe anthropology and communication are approaches, not bodies of data, and that within each the four winds of the humanities, the physical, the biological and the social sciences intermingle to form a science of man.

Volumes 1 through 6:

Editor:
    E. S. Carpenter
Associate Editors:
    W. T. Easterbrook
    H. M. McLuhan
    J. Tyrwhitt
    D. C. Williams

Address all correspondence to EXPLORATIONS
 University of Toronto
 Toronto, Canada

Volumes 7 & 8:

Editors:
    Edmund Carpenter
    Marshall McLuhan

Sponsor Telegram of Toronto
Publisher University of Toronto

February 1955

Explorations, 1953–57

Foreword to the Eight-Volume Series of the 2016 Edition, Volumes 2–8

(The main Introduction to this series is in Volume One)

Michael Darroch (University of Windsor) and
Janine Marchessault (York University)

Explorations was an experimental interdisciplinary publication led by faculty and graduate students at the University of Toronto in which the media theorist Marshall McLuhan and the radical anthropologist Edmund Carpenter formulated their most striking insights about new media in the electric age. The journal served to disseminate some of the insights and experiments of the Culture and Communications graduate seminar (1953–55), an innovative media think tank of the 1950s. The eight coedited issues of *Explorations* are republished here for the first time since their original printing in the 1950s.

The Explorations research group aimed to develop a "field approach" to the study of new media and communication. While inspired by a postwar, modernist discourse of universality, no single mode of research was dominant. By their own account, the team sought "an area of mutually supporting insights in a critique of the methods of study in Economics, Psychology, English, Anthropology, and Town Planning."[1] *Explorations* published writings by group

---

1. Herbert Marshall McLuhan Fonds, held in Library and Archives Canada (LAC) in Ottawa. Further references to the McLuhan Fonds will be identified as LAC followed by the call number MG 31, D 156, the volume number, and the folder number (here: LAC MG 31, D 156, 145, 35).

members along with contributions on topics ranging from ethnolinguistics to economic theory, from art and design to developmental psychology, from psychoanalysis to nursery rhymes and bawdy ballads, from urban theory to electronic media. The journal treated culture, and cultural studies, as a landscape of experiences and knowledge. An experimental space in its own right, *Explorations* counted among its more than eighty contributors both established and emerging scholars, scientists, and artists.

The think tank and the journal were supported by a grant from the Ford Foundation's newly established interdisciplinary research and study program in behavioral sciences (most likely cowritten by McLuhan and Carpenter and assisted by the then doctoral student Donald Theall). The group obtained $44,250 for a two-year research project devoted to studying the "changing patterns of language and behavior and the new media of communication."[2] Within North America, the Toronto group's proposal can be counted among the very first attempts to combine explicitly the study of culture *and* communication. The timing of this grant is significant given the scope of contemporaneous studies of media underway in the United States and Europe: functionalist and critical cultural studies of mass communications, theories of cybernetics, studies of social interaction, as well as psychological studies of the effects of media on human perception. Carpenter, initially the driving force behind *Explorations*, acted as editor of the first six issues before becoming coeditor with McLuhan for issues 7 and 8, which were sponsored by the *Toronto Telegram*. A ninth and final issue, entitled *Eskimo* (1959), combined Carpenter's writings on indigenous art and culture of the Aivilik juxtaposed with images from filmmaker Robert Flaherty and drawings by Frederick Varley. After Beacon Press published a selection of *Explorations* contributions in 1960, coedited by Carpenter and McLuhan as *Explorations in Communication*, McLuhan later resuscitated the spirit of *Explorations* as a "magazine within a magazine," a publication inside the University of Toronto's alumni magazine, the *Varsity Graduate* (1964–72).

2. *Ford Foundation, 1953, Ford Foundation Annual Report 1953*, New York: Ford Foundation: 67. The Ford Foundation's Behavioral Sciences Program had the stated goal of "improving the content of the behavioral sciences" by specifically supporting "interdisciplinary research and study." Launched in 1952, the program aimed to help the "intellectual development of the behavioral sciences" by "improving their relationship with such disciplines as history, social and political philosophy, humanistic studies and certain phases of economics" (67).

The group's proposal to Ford's Behavioral Sciences Program is revealing of the central assumptions that would underpin the graduate seminar and *Explorations*. The proposal's point of departure is not yet an assumption about the power of media forms to shape content, but rather the understanding that methods for studying new media required recognition of new patterns emerging across technological, cultural, and urban life. Underpinning the proposal is a conversation that McLuhan in particular had started with advocates of cybernetic theories. Carpenter was also of course conversant with the writings of anthropologists who were deeply involved with developing cybernetic models and metaphors within the social sciences, among others Gregory Bateson and Margaret Mead. Cybernetic theories also came to the group through Donald Theall, who would complete his PhD dissertation in 1954 on "Communication Theories in Modern Poetry: Yeats, Pound, Joyce and Eliot" under the supervision of both McLuhan and Carpenter.

"Well aware of the brilliant new developments in communication study at Massachusetts Institute of Technology," the Ford grant explains, gesturing both to Norbert Wiener's cybernetic conferences and to Claude Shannon and Warren Weaver's mathematical theory of communication, "the undersigned propose to utilize these insights but to employ also the technique of studying the forms of communication, old and new, as art forms," an approach already "implicit in the very title of Harold Innis' *Bias of Communication*."[3] The Toronto group proposed to study the effects of new media forms on patterns of language, economic values, social organization, individual and collective behaviour, always keeping in mind accompanying changes to the classroom and the networks of city life. In their eyes the central problem consisted of two aspects. First, "the creation of a new language of vision" that "arises from all our new visual media and which is part of the total language of modern culture." Second, the Toronto group proposed to study "the impact of this total social language on the traditional spoken and written forms of expression." These two core objectives they would pursue in the pages of *Explorations* through numerous contributions. As clearly indicated in an early draft of their Ford proposal, the core research group

3. Edmund S. Carpenter, Jaqueline Tyrwhitt, H. M. McLuhan, W. T. Easterbrook, and D. C. Williams, 1953, "University of Toronto: Changing Patterns of Language and Behavior and the New Media of Communication." Ford Foundation Archives. Grant File PA 53–70, Section 1, 1–11. Rockefeller Archive Center, New York: 4.

represented the five key disciplines that would supplement each other: anthropology, psychology, economics, town planning, and English.[4]

While no one discipline was privileged above the others, anthropology played a special role in creating a strong comparative framework from the start. In addition to anthropological discussions of cybernetics, the Sapir-Whorf theory was an important intellectual foundation. As with Innis, Edward Sapir (a German-born American who spent fifteen years in Ottawa working for the Geographical Survey of Canada) offered a multifocal habit of vision, working between linguistics, anthropology, and psychology. For the grant applicants, Sapir "brought together European attitudes towards psychoanalysis (emphasis on socially-situated personality) and North American attitudes towards social structure (culture)." Moreover, Sapir "fused the European concern with philology with [the] North American concern with dynamic patterns in language."[5] The anthropologist and ethnolinguist Dorothy Lee was arguably one of the group's "most influential force[s],"[6] contributing six articles on language, value, and perception. Her insight that peoples such as the Trobrianders perceived lineal order differently from Western cultures had already been cited by Bateson and Ruesch (1951), and was central to the delineation of acoustic and visual cultures undertaken by the Explorations group, and in later studies by both McLuhan and Carpenter.

In developing their methodologies, seminar faculty and graduate students undertook a number of critical media experiments on changing patterns of perception resulting from new media. The CBC and the then Ryerson Institute placed studio space and media equipment at their disposal. The experiment tested their central hypothesis that different media (speech, print, radio, television) lend themselves to different kinds of pedagogical experiences.[7] It is surprising that such findings have never been fully taken up by educational media researchers. Hopefully, the republication of these early studies will

4. "Changing Patterns of Man and Society Associated with the New Media of Communication." Draft of Ford Foundation Proposal, likely 1953. LAC MG 31, D 156, 204, 26.

5. Carpenter et al, 1953: 2.

6. Edmund Carpenter, 2001, "That Not-So-Silent Sea," in Donald F. Theall (Ed.), *The Virtual Marshall McLuhan* (p. 240), Montreal: McGill-Queen's University Press.

7. Edmund Carpenter, 1954, "Certain Media Biases," *Explorations* 3:65–74; Edmund Carpenter and Marshall McLuhan, 1956, "The New Languages," *Chicago Review* 10(1): 46–52; Edmund Carpenter, 1957, "The New Languages," *Explorations* 7:4–21.

renew interest in the cognitive studies of media which have focussed too narrowly, according to Carpenter and McLuhan, on attention and inputs and not enough on the creative and critical aspects of perception.

What is clear in reading through the *Explorations* issues is that Carpenter and McLuhan were most interested in the new kinds of learning made possible through the media. McLuhan, in particular, was influenced by research into human perception as part of his approach to media studies since he believed that these media were altering our senses, our forms of attention and knowledge production. Carpenter and McLuhan would assert that the media are transforming the human sensorium, an idea captured perhaps most playfully in the final coedited issue, *Explorations* 8, an ode to James Joyce devoted to the oral, to the new "acoustic space" of the electric age: "Verbi-Voco-Visual." The issue features seven essays, including one by McLuhan, that explore different aspects of oral culture—mostly concerned with a transition to a new orality. Twenty-four non-authored "Items," which include some previously published essays by McLuhan and Carpenter, appear as humorous intellectual sketches exploring topics like "Electronics as ESP," car commercials, bathroom acoustics, dictaphones, and of course wine. The final "Item," number 24, entitled "No Upside Down in Eskimo Art," reiterated McLuhan and Carpenter's core assertion that "after thousands of years of written processing of human experience, the instantaneous omnipresence of electronically processed information has hoicked us out of these age-old patterns into an auditory world." In the history of media studies in Canada and internationally, the *Explorations* journal is an important starting point for defining the rich new insights around new media cultures that the Toronto School helped inaugurate.

References

Carpenter, Edmund S., Jaqueline Tyrwhitt, H. M. McLuhan, W. T. Easterbrook, and D. C. Williams. 1953. "University of Toronto: Changing Patterns of Language and Behavior and the New Media of Communication." Ford Foundation Archives. Grant File PA 53–70, Section 1, 1–11. Rockefeller Archive Center, New York.

Carpenter, Edmund. 1954. "Certain Media Biases." *Explorations* 3:65–74.

Carpenter, Edmund. 1957. "The New Languages." *Explorations* 7:4–21.

Carpenter, Edmund. 2001. "That Not-So-Silent Sea." In Donald F. Theall (Ed.), *The Virtual Marshall McLuhan* (pp. 236–61). Montreal: McGill-Queen's University Press.

Carpenter, Edmund, and Marshall McLuhan. 1956. "The New Languages." *Chicago Review* 10(1): 46–52.

Ford Foundation. 1953. *Ford Foundation Annual Report 1953*. New York: Ford Foundation.

Ruesch, Jurgen, and Gregory Bateson. 1951. *Communication, the Social Matrix of Psychiatry*. New York: Norton.

Theall, Donald. 1954. *Communication Theories in Modern Poetry: Yeats, Pound, Eliot and Joyce*. Doctoral dissertation. Toronto: University of Toronto.

Summaries of All Eight
Explorations Volumes

Explorations 1

Explorations 1 took an audaciously new approach to communications and cultural research "cutting across" studies in anthropology, literature, social sciences, economics, folklore, and popular culture. From Copernican revolutions (Bidney) to a seventeenth-century translation of Sweden's Mohra witchcraft trials (Horneck); from senses of time (Leach) to the meaning of gongs (Carrington); from Majorcan customs (Graves) to a typography of functional analysis (Spiro); from Veblen's economic history (Riesman) to contemporary stress levels (Selye), the issue also included one of György Kepes's earliest drafts on fusing "art and science," an essay on Freud and vices (Goodman), and a return to childhood in Legman's work on comic books, before concluding with now classic essays by McLuhan and Frye. The cover of *Explorations* 1 depicts a series of masks from the award-winning film *The Loon's Necklace* (Crawley Films, 1948).

Explorations 2

Explorations 2's mischievous spoof covers, both front and back, inside and outside, were labelled "Feenicht's Playhouse," a reference to the Phoenix playhouse of Joyce's *Wake*. The key playful headline, "New Media Changing Temporal and Spatial Orientation to Self," was accompanied by multiple hoax articles, including "Time-Space Duality Goes" and "TV Wollops MS," a reference to television's apparent power over manuscript culture as evidenced by the group's media experiment at CBC studios. Exemplifying the playfulness of the core faculty's discussions about new media and behaviour, it is not surprising the McLuhan would publish in this issue his now famous article "Notes on the Media as Art Forms" alongside essays by other seminar participants: Tyrwhitt resuscitated an unpublished article, "Ideal Cities and the City Ideal," a historical survey of proposals for ideal urban designs (originally drafted for the defunct journal *trans/formation: art, communication, environment*). Carpenter's "Eternal Life" is a first analysis of Aivilik Inuit concepts of time; then student Donald Theall's "Here Comes Everybody" offered a snapshot of his research on Joyce and communication theories in modern poetry; anthropologist Dorothy Lee, who would visit the seminar in March 1955, offered a review of David Bidney's challenge to scholarly traditions in his 1953 book *Theoretical Anthropology*. In addition, Carpenter fleshed out the contents with contributions from political economy, anthropology, psychology, and English: the second part of Riesman's Veblen study; Lord Raglan on social classes; Derek Savage on "Jung, Alchemy and Self"; the *New Yorker*'s Stanley Hyman on Malraux's thesis of the "museum without walls"; and A. Irving Hallowell's extended essay on "Self and its Behavioral Environment"—the inspiration for the spoof cover.

Explorations 3

Explorations 3 was initially planned as a volume dedicated to Harold Innis. In the end, the issue would only include Innis's essay "Monopoly and Civilization," introduced by Easterbrook, and a series of reflections in "Innis and Communication" by seminar participants. In November 1954, the *Explorations* researchers attended the "Institute on Culture and Communication" organised by Ray Birdwhistell at the University of Louisville's Interdisciplinary Committee on Culture and Communication. A number of the contributions to *Explorations* 3 are essays or early drafts of contributions related to this conference (Birdwhistell, Lee, Trager & Hall). The issue also includes the initial, and substantially divergent, assessments of the group's first "media experiment" at CBC studios (April 1954) in the contributions by Carpenter and Williams. The issue is rounded out with an excerpt on reading and writing (Chaytor), a new translation of Kamo Chomei's *Hojoki* (Rowe & Kerrigan), a study of utopias (Wolfenstein), a reading of *Tristram Shandy* (MacLean), reflections on Soviet ethnography (Potekin & Levin), a reading of Shelley's hallucinations as narcissism and doublegoing (McCullough), a critical reassessment of the science of human behaviour (Wallace), and "Meat Packing and Processing," an anonymous entry, likely by McLuhan, alluding to Giedion's *Mechanization Takes Command* (1948). Like *Explorations* 1, the cover depicted an indigenous mask from the Northwest Coast also represented in the Crawley film *The Loon's Necklace* (1948).

Explorations 4

According to McLuhan, *Explorations* 4 was planned as an issue devoted to Sigfried Giedion. Published in February 1955, with a cover adapted from Kandinsky's *Comets* (1938), *Explorations* 4 was devoted to issues of space and placed a strong emphasis on modes of linguistic and poetic thought across multiple media. Poems by e. e. cummings and Jorge Luis Borges mingle with essays by seminar leaders McLuhan on "Space, Time, and Poetry," Carpenter on "Eskimo Poetry: Word Magic," Tyrwhitt on "The Moving Eye" (regarding comparative perceptual experiences of Western cities and the ancient Indian city of Fatehpur Sikri), and Williams on "auditory space"—a notion that "electrified" the group, as Carpenter later recounted. Northrop Frye and Stephen Gilman's essays on poetic traditions were juxtaposed with Millar MacLure and Marjorie Adix's odes to Dylan Thomas, who had died in 1953. Case studies by then graduate students Walter J. Ong on "Space in Renaissance Symbolism" and Joan Rayfield on "Implications of English Grammar" were aligned with Dorothy Lee's contribution on "Freedom, Spontaneity and Limit in American Linguistic Usage" and Lawrence Frank's early draft of "Tactile Communication." Both Lee and Frank had presented their contributions at Ray Birdwhistell's "Institute on Culture and Communication" in Louisville, in 1954. A "Media Log" and the now famous entry "Five Sovereign Fingers Taxed the Breath," both largely replicated from McLuhan's 1954 *Counterblast* pamphlet, were published anonymously. In addition to "Our Enchanted Lives," a memorandum of instructions for television programming adapted from a Procter & Gamble memo, "The Party Line" offered a second alleged memorandum "To All TIME INC. Bureaus and Stringers." An "Idea File" containing insights on oral, written, and technological cultural forms was culled from writings by Robert Graves, Edmund Leach, Walter Gropius, and E. T. Hall, among many others. With *Explorations* 4, the group revealed its commitment to the belief that communication studies was deeply rooted in anthropological and literary-poetic traditions, but equally informed by studies of mechanisation, technology, and culture.

Explorations 5

The cover of *Explorations* 5 returned to the playfulness of issue 2: the image of the famous Minoan "Our Lady of the Sports" figurine, held at the Royal Ontario Museum (the authenticity of which has long been disputed) was set in front of the *Toronto Daily Star*'s 8 April 1954 Home Edition front page, featuring the headline "H-Bomb in Mass Production, U.S." This juxtaposition between ancient artefact, contemporary media, and techno-logical production set the stage for the issue: starting with Daisetz Suzuki's description of "Buddhist Symbolism", the issue follows with McLuhan's famous analysis of TV and radio in Joyce's *Finnegans Wake*. Such contrasts of new media forms continue with a "Portrait of James Joyce," an excerpt of a 1950 "Third Programme" BBC documentary edited by W. R. Rodgers, and the two-page "Anna Livia Plurabelle" section of Joyce's *Finnegans Wake*, set in experimental typography designed by Harley Parker and Toronto's Cooper and Beatty Ltd. The issue further juxtaposes essays by E. R. Leach on cultural conceptions of time and Jean Piaget on time-space conceptions of the child; anthropologists Claire Holt and Joan Rayfield on interpen-etrations of language and culture and Carpenter's study of Eskimo space concepts; Rhodra Métraux on differences between the novel, play, and film versions of *The Caine Mutiny*; Roy Campbell on the fusion of oral and writ-ten traditions in the writings of Nigerian author Amos Tutuola, including an excerpt of his 1954 novel *My Life in the Bush of Ghosts*, and Harcourt Brown on Pascal; economist Kenneth Boulding on information theory and Easterbrook on economic approaches to communication; and an excerpt from Daniel Lerner and David Riesman's work on the modernisation of Turkey and the Middle East. Tyrwhitt and Williams contributed reflec-tions on the seminar's second media experiment in "The City Unseen," an analysis of students' perceptions of the environment of the then Ryerson Institute. Anonymous entries included "Colour and Communication" and a transcription of satirist Jean Shepherd's radio broadcast "Channel Cat in the Middle Distance," likely courtesy of Carpenter. The issue is rounded out with a Letters File and an Ideas File, with contributions from E. R. Leach, Patrick Geddes, and Lawrence Frank.

Explorations 6

Writing to the Explorations Group in 1954, Carpenter worried about the funds from the Ford grant that were available for publishing this issue. *Explorations* 6 was funded through the sales of issue 5 and possibly Carpenter's own funds. The cover image for this issue was a section of *The Great Wave*, by Katsushika Hokusai. According to Carpenter's letter, this issue summarizes the group's "ideas and findings," which though "not fully articulated" were "new and exciting." He saw the issue as "a full seminar statement." Indeed, the issue brings together the interdisciplinary reflections and comparative media studies that characterized the group's methodology: a brilliant essay by radical anthropologist Dorothy Lee on "Wintu thought" (Lee would ultimately publish six essays in *Explorations* and had a significant influence on the seminar) and two essays on television that were solicited to reflect upon different geographical differences that shaped the experiences of the new medium—one in the US (Chayefsky) and the other the Soviet Union (Sharoyeva, the "top man" in the USSR television system). Also included were Giedion's classic essay on cave painting; a reflection on the phonograph alongside a consideration of "print's monopoly" by C. S. Lewis; as well as essays by McLuhan on media and events; language and magic (Maritain); writing and orality (Riesman); color (Parker); the evolution of the human mind (Montagu); and the anonymous entries "Print's Monopoly" and "Feet of Clay," likely drafted by McLuhan and Carpenter, which take up conflicts between old and new media environments. This issue contains the full spectrum of the weekly seminar's research undertakings over a two-year period.

Explorations 7

Explorations 7 (1957), the only issue without a table of contents, was edited by Carpenter and McLuhan solely and, with issue 8, sponsored by the *Toronto Telegram*. Easterbrook and Tyrwhitt were away, and Williams wanted his name taken off the masthead, allegedly because of the publication of American writer Gershon Legman's infamous "Bawdy Song . . . in Fact and in Print," a history of erotic writing. McLuhan had contributed to Legman's short-lived but hugely influential magazine *Neurotica* (1948–52), so the two had a previous connection. But the tension between Williams and the editors might have also been due to their different interpretations of the CBC/Ryerson media experiments which explored media sensory biases with a group of students discussed in issue 3 by Williams in scientific terms, and here again by Carpenter in his essay "The New Languages" in cultural terms. Carpenter argues that each medium (radio, TV, print) "codifies reality differently." To accompany this opening essay, they each included anonymous entries: the essay "Classroom Without Walls," later attributed to McLuhan, explores the ubiquitous mediasphere outside educational institutions, which teachers must begin to consider as an inherent and unavoidable pedagogical experience, followed by "Songs of the Pogo," a reference to the popular comic and LP of the period, which pervaded the McLuhan home. McLuhan saw relationships between "Jazz and Modern Letters," juxtaposed with Carpenter's reflections on the acoustic character of ancient and preliterate symbols, masks, and traditions in "Eternal Life of the Dream." Dorothy Lee contributed two essays to the issue on lineal and non-lineal codifications examined in the Trobriand language with responses by Robert Graves. The focus on educational matters also included a review of Riesman's *Variety and Constraint in American Education* as well as examinations of the cultural specificity of the Soviet press, Soviet novels, and Soviet responses to Elvis Presley. The particularity of an oral and noncapitalistic culture had been an important point of comparison for the Explorations Group, especially Carpenter and McLuhan. Harley Parker designed the issue's cover.

Explorations 8

Explorations 8 (1957) is perhaps the most famous of all the issues. It was devoted to the oral—"Verbi-Voco-Visual"—and was edited primarily by McLuhan and again published by the *Toronto Telegram* and the University of Toronto. The issue was filled with visual experimentation; framed by extensive play with typography in the spirit of the Vorticists and for the first time the extensive use of "flexitype" by Harley Parker, then display designer at the ROM. Seen throughout are Parker's experiments with typography as well as color printing, the first time in the history of the journal. A photomontage from László Moholy-Nagy's *Vision in Motion* (1947) depicting a man's face with an ear juxtaposed over an eye is the frontispiece to the issue. The issue features seven essays, including one by McLuhan, that explore different aspects of oral culture—mostly concerned with a transition to a new orality. Twenty-four non-authored "Items," which include some previously published essays by McLuhan and Carpenter, appear as humorous intellectual sketches exploring topics like "Electronics as ESP," car commercials, bathroom acoustics, dictaphones, and of course wine. The final "Item," number 24, entitled "No Upside Down in Eskimo Art," reiterated McLuhan and Carpenter's core assertion that "after thousands of years of written processing of human experience, the instantaneous omnipresence of electronically processed information has hoicked us out of these age-old patterns into an auditory world."

Michael Darroch (University of Windsor)
Janine Marchessault (York University)
2016

VOLUME 4

The study I present here began as a search for linguistic clues to American concepts pertaining to freedom and the self.[1] It soon seemed to me significant that certain usages were appearing increasingly in the speech and the writings of a cross-section of the American people, even though these usages were not considered good English, and were therefore under attack, or at any rate not encouraged, in the schools. Of these, I chose to concentrate on the verbal *up* in relation to the verbal *out* (as in *sign up, open up, write out, figure out*), and on a term used for relating the subject to his situation: the *have to* (or *got to* or *have got to*). I saw the verbal *up* as a means of stressing the given limit of the act, and as an expression of the absence of the quality of randomness or exploration in the activity of the self. The *have to* seemed to me to relate the individual to his situation in terms of compulsion, of an absence of choice. Both of these showed, to my mind, that freedom and spontaneity were decreasing, at any rate as values, in American society, and that the desire for limit was increasing.

A brief search for terms such as *free* and *freedom* confirmed me in my suspicion. I found *free* used in connection with free from schedule ('free time' or 'I am free to see you now'); and free from pay, ('free

[1] Based on a pilot study into linguistic clues to American concepts and values, undertaken under the auspices of the Rockefeller Foundation, Division of Humanities.

cigars', 'the best things in life are free'). Occasionally, I found it used in connection with freedom from entanglement ('he is free', *i.e.*, un-married). Otherwise, it was used almost exclusively by politicians, social scientists and leaders in general. This seemed to imply a lack of interest in inner freedom. The freedom of the self was apparently not an American value. With unscientific absence of detachment, I found this distressing.

In this essay, I shall speak mainly of my inquiry into the meaning of the verbal *up*, into its use, and into the nature of the clue it furnishes.

My first concern was to assess my clue, to find out exactly how the *up* was used, with what verbs, in what situations, by whom and to whom. I made a cursory examination of the history of its use through the material given in Murray's *New English Dictionary*. In addition, I analysed ten American plays from the eighteenth and nineteenth centuries, and a few English sources for comparison. From the twentieth century, and particularly from the last ten years, I have analysed material from a great variety of sources. Much of this comes from conversations recorded by participants or observers, and from the transcription of tape-recorded speech. Approximately an equal amount comes from conversations in plays and novels, and from other written sources. In general, the written material is of the type where communication is attempted, and the audience is presumably alive in the writer's consciousness; for ex-ample, from popular magazines, sports columns in the newspapers, answers to questions as in high school quizzes, letters seeking help, and other similar sources. The study suffers in that at no time could I take into account the total context of speech; of the tone of voice, the kinesic components, the evocative response of the hearer; nor do I have a record of the pitch accent of the *up*. Some context is here: the audience —hearer or reader—; the situation, whether a conservative classroom, or the 'permissive' atmosphere of the counselor's office, or the milieu estab-lished by the author in the novel or play. And to some extent, I tried to 'control' the context; if I examined essays of children from a conservative school, I also examined those from a progressive school; if I analysed compositions, I also analysed quizzes which were anticipated by the students and quizzes which were announced suddenly without time for preparation. I examined stress interviews as well as non-directive ones.

In making a study of the *up* I limited myself to those words whose essential denotation did not depend on the *up*. I did not include cases where, to omit the up, would have meant substituting another verb. For example, in saying 'make up your mind', if the speaker wants to refrain from using the *up*, he cannot use the *make* alone, but choose *decide*

2

instead. This is true of many words, such as 'make up my face', 'give up', 'turn up', usually words old in English usage. I also omitted all occasions when the *up* definitely referred to an upward motion as in *get up* (in the morning), or to motion toward a physical point as in *walked up* (to him). The instances I do include are those where the individual chooses, as for example, between *lock* and *lock up;* where the *up* changes the feeling tone of the verb, or, rather—since it is necessary to be more vague—refers to something beyond what the verb itself conveys. I cannot characterize or categorize this 'something'. I began by calling it an aspect of the verb, and ended by trying to call it a mood; but its nature resists the application of a name so undynamic as mood.

Examination of verbs to which the *up* was attached in comparison to verbs without the *up* showed me that the *up* stressed activity coming to definite end and in a brief time; that is, it emphasized quick results. For example, *write* directs to a process vague as to result or time involved; *write (it) up* means bring it to a definite, clear end, expeditiously. Contrast *write it up* to *write it out*, for example;—I can say write it out carefully, or slowly; but I cannot use these adverbs with *write it up;* I can say, instead, 'I'll *write it up* in a jiffy.'

Beyond this, it became apparent that the *up* expressed something valued; that the limit was desired and good. For example, words ending in *up* were more good, had a higher prestige, than those ending in *around,* such as *to fool around,* or as in: 'I was just *looking around.*' These non-purposive, limitless terms, were at the further end of the value scale from *up,* along with the valueless words which denote activity without defined purpose or limit, such as those ending in *er or le: fritter* or *putter* or *fiddle* or *flounder* or *whittle;* terms so definitely valueless, that one of the questions which my children had to answer in a standard questionnaire, ran something like this: which is the more worthwhile occupation, whittling or carving?

Words ending in *up* I found to be in clear contrast to these value-lacking terms. The *up* was being used not only to delineate activity, but to point to activity purposefully undertaken with a view to reaching the limit, the results. The difference between *to clean* and *to clean up,* *to fix* and *to fix up,* I saw as one of end in the sense of both limit and goal. The speed also implied in this *up,* I considered a stress on the straight line as the shortest course to the goal. When the emphasis was on process, I saw that the *up* could not be used; we do not *loiter up,* nor do we *play up dominoes.*

Reference to Murray's *New English Dictionary* showed that the verbal use of the *up* is not new in English. Since the tenth century, the *up* alone, not as postposition, has been in use to indicate the physical or temporal limit of the act; as, for example, in: *up to dam brigge* (up to the bridge); and since the fourteenth, it has been used postpositionally in this sense, as in: *we gon up to Jerusalem.* Since that time, it has also been used in the resultative sense. In the *New English Dictionary,* I also find an instance from the fifteenth century which implies that the factor of speed may already be present: *polished up thy work in goodly tyme.* However, the terms listed as ending in the *up* are not always acceptable to the present-day reader, even though their stress may be, as today, on the result. For example, we find here: *he died up, he resigned up, to surrender up, the yield up of the land.* If the deciding factor in the use of the *up* is the presence of end or result, then why does it seem strange to find the *up* used with these words?

To find out what else was expressed in the *up,* I compared it to the verbal *out,* which also appeared to me to point to the completion of an activity. On the surface, the main difference between the two seemed to be that, as I mentioned above, whereas the *up* emphasized speed, a straight line to the end, the *out* emphasized the process. I say, for instance, *clean it up fast,* but *clean it out carefully; burn it up quickly,* but *let it burn out thoroughly.* I *think up* something on the spur of the moment, but I *think it out* slowly or gradually. However, my diagnosis of the meaning of *up* did not satisfy me when I came to the last doublet; the difference between *up* and *out* goes here beyond mere stress on process. In contrast to the *out,* the *up* here contains an element of personal decisiveness, of creativeness, of spontaneity. When you *think up,* you invent, or at any rate, you bring forth something unique to yourself, even when this is nothing but an excuse to avoid blame. With this in mind, I noticed that this meaning of the *up* was predominant in a number of expressions, such as: *to come up* with an idea, or *to speak up* or *to stand up for* my convictions.

Upon re-examination of my material, it appeared that this meaning of the *up* was actually present to some extent in all the instances of the postpositional use of the *up.* It is difficult to define this meaning. It involves spontaneity; yet this is not the spontaneity that we associate with freedom. It is the taking of a step; it involves a decisive act of the self. I do not use the term assertive to describe it since that implies awareness of another, a turning toward another; and in the *up* I believe only the self is stressed, not the act or the acted upon. What is expressed is rather a personal application of the self. For example, even in a term low in the degree of self involvement stressed, such as *clean up* or *lock up,* the *lock up* implies to some extent, 'I'll personally see to it that it is locked.'

In one sense, it gives calibre and strength to a vague activity—the *up* puts the American quality of guts into the act. This, I think, is why the older terms such as *surrender up* or *die up* are unacceptable now; they are self-contradictory. Nowadays, *I die up* only if I apply myself to comitting psychosomatic suicide.

The *up* of spontaneity has actually been in use for centuries. In its stronger meaning, it has stood alone with a verbal connotation; from the sixteenth century we have: *he up with a long circumstance, they up and declare.* Without more intensive study, I cannot say whether this meaning is present in the postpositional *up* as used in this century. It does not seem to be present in the long excerpts I read from *Pendennis* and *Moll Flanders.* In ten American plays from 1714 to 1852, I found it only twice.

Another element in the meaning of the *up,* one more clearly limited to this century, and more clearly on the increase, is the reversal of the activity of the actor upon himself. This sometimes seems merely to detransitivize a given word, turning the act upon the self, making it what we might have called a middle, in other circumstances. *Bear up* is the earliest such expression I found in American literature so far, in a play written in 1824. Apart from the case of *brighten up* in *Alice in Wonderland,* this is the only instance I found before the twentieth century. Now the use of the *up* in this sense is relatively frequent. We say '*I open up*', '*I warm up*', '*They lined up against the fence.*' We use these expressions in place of: *I warmed myself, we lined ourselves, I opened myself to her.* So far it seems as if the *up* merely changes a reflexive into a middle. Yet what is present here is not the acquiescence or receptivity of the middle; in extreme cases what we find is obviously quite the opposite. Take the recent expression to *meet up with,* for example. This I have found in conversation, in classroom discussion, and in learned writing, since I first noticed it in 1950. The *up* detransitivizes the *meet,* but it does not devitalize it; it makes it more vigorous. It takes the emphasis away from the relationship with the met, the acted upon, and turns it upon the actor. The *up* refers here, not so much to the limit of the act but to the actor himself, showing him to be more highly agentive than the mere *meet* does. In effect it emphasizes the agentive quality of the actor at the expense of the transitivity of the act.

The new words detransitivized through the postposition *up* are few, but they are significant. *To join up with,* for example, incorporates more of the self than the plain *to join.* Where the *join* may be an act of mere conformity, the *join up with* implies to some degree an act of personal will, and of self involvement. Perhaps the expression which holds this connotation most clearly is *face up to.* Apparently to *face* alone was not felt to be strong enough. In the last ten or fifteen years, *face up to* is used with increasing frequency, and now *face up to* is used by people of strong convictions, speaking with a sense of sincerity and personal responsibility. Here the *up* carries much of the strength of the independent *up*, as in: *he up and faced it.* I have heard this term used by a professor of education when describing starvation in the streets of Tokyo. I have heard John Collier say, while speaking of the creative spirit: 'We are trying to meet life, to face up to life.' I read the expression in a paper by John Gillin, speaking of a difficult situation relating to public school education. Here, again, the *up* means the calling forth of courage and a mobilization of the self rising to meet a challenge.

Now, if there was an increase of the personal relatedness of the self to the situation, this should be evident elsewhere in the language. At this point of my study I turned back to the *out*. The *out* has never been used as much as the *up*; though, as in *dies out*, it is listed for 1420 in the *New English Dictionary*. Until recent years, the emphasis of *out* was upon a long process of completion or depletion. It occurs in phrases such as: *patience to hear you out; he wrote it out laboriously; I finally wore it out.* Yet, to go back to our comparison of *think up*, and *think out*:— if the *up* actually implied that the thought had to be brought into existence, what did the *out* mean? It meant that the thought was already there. The statement, the logical proposition was present and known; it was a given. The *out*, I think, refers to the completion or depletion of an actualized given. So: I *carry out* a given order; when I am *tired out*, I have used up my given energy; when I die, I have *lived out* the span of my life; when I *measure out* the sugar, I limit myself to what is there, or to the appropriate amount established by the recipe book, and stop where that ends.

So far this indicates no increase of personal involvement. However, a recent development in its use does point to a personalization of the *out*. The *out* is being used, increasingly, in the verbs dealing with thinking and reflection. I find only one record of such use in the *New English Dictionary*, and no instances in the literature I examined, dating before 1928. Since then, the commonest use of *out* is with the words *work* and *figure*, as in *figure out*, and *work out*. This term occurs in a wide range of situations: in counseling interviews, where in a course of non-directive therapy the *out* with reflective words may occur as much as fifteen times as often as with verbs having a physical reference; and in a book packed with as much action as *I Can Get It For You Wholesale*. If the *out* does represent the actualization of the given, then this new use of the *out* is another indication of the agentive vigour of the self; it suggests that the individual does not accept the given blindly, but now applies

6

himself to it in a spirit of inquiry; he *puzzles it out,* he *works it out,* he *thrashes it out,* he *figures it out.*

I found corroboration for the assumption of this growing spirit of personal inquiry in another linguistic usage. The use of the *must* in recent years has been mainly limited to a reference to logical necessity; that is the speaker uses the *must* as a way of *figuring out* the given. In *Macbeth,* out of thirty occurrences of *must,* I find no occurrence of the *must* of logical necessity. Throughout the nineteenth century, I find it both in English and American literature; but in this country, the occurrences of the *must* of logical necessity increase and soon outnumber the use of the other *must*; whereas, in my little reading of English literature through the nineteenth century, I find the opposite to be true for England. This development, then, is recent, and mainly American; and it is, I should say, another indication that the American individual does not merely accept the given, but applies himself personally to it; that he tries to *figure it out.*

I concluded from all this that the *up* does not refer merely to limit, as I thought at the start of my inquiry. It refers to a personally chosen end, an end to which the individual applies himself with decisiveness and vigour. Speed is a part of its meaning; but as part of it, it is not merely a temporal quality. It is now a quality of the person, of upsurging strength. Perhaps it contains something of the meaning of quickening, which identifies speed and life. Freedom, on the other hand, is not in the picture; it is the limit which provides backbone which evokes the personal involvement of the individual, in terms of motivation and spontaneity. In fact, when this limit is absent the response of quickening does not seem to occur.

I had begun my inquiry into the *up* with a feeling that I would not like what it led me to. I had considered the limit contained in the meaning of the *up* as restricting and depriving. I found it, instead, challenging and motivating toward temporary enhancement of the self, calling out an answering upsurge of the self. I found it the expression of the peculiarly American version of spontaneity and vigour.

An exploratory study was next attempted to find out what are the factors underlying the use of the *up* by a specific individual, or in a specific situation; or, to phrase it according to my conclusions, what situations challenge an individual to a responding mobilization of the self and what kind of person does an individual have to be to recognize and rise to the challenge.

This exploratory study has only suggested lines of investigation so far. For example, analysis of non-directive counseling material indicates a less frequent use of the *up* in proportion to the use of the verbal *out,* than is common elsewhere (37 *up* to 32 *out* in one series of interviews; 58 *up* to 20 *out* in another series; whereas in two plays from 1950, I find 36 *up* to 8 *out* and 22 *up* to 1 *out*). Does this mean that a permissive situation does not evoke in the individual a response of vigour? A parallel investigation of compositions of children in a progressive school in comparison with those of children in a conservative public junior high school was attempted as a possible control; and here the *up* was found to be more frequent in the former group of compositions. The progressive school, however, was not non-directive in its approach. It was permissive in the sense that it allowed children to use language as they knew it; whereas the conservative school was opposed to the use of *up*, as not good English, that is, it provided restriction not challenge. So that I found that when children in a structured situation were allowed to use the verbal *up*, they did use it. On the other hand, the counseling situation, like the progressive school, also afforded the freedom to use speech according to the speaker's wish; yet the speaker did not choose to use the *up* frequently. I remained with the question: was it the situation that did not evoke the response of *up*? or was it the individual who, in self-doubt and conflict, could not respond in terms of *up*? That it may be the individual, is suggested by the following: twice when one of the speakers used the *up* of spontaneity or creativity, she qualified it with an apologetic or belittling *just* 'something I *just* built *up* myself'. In opposing the individual to the situation here, I merely want to emphasize shift of focus; I do not mean to separate the one from the other.

In children's books the verbal *up* is curiously rare or absent, though the language used is a simple vernacular and other postpositions such as the verbal *over* or *through* are present. This is the case also with the writing in popular magazines, pulps, popular Sunday supplements. Even the whipped up vernacular of the sports pages which I investigated, rarely, if ever, makes use of the verbal *up*. Does this mean that the self is not fully mobilized when we address ourselves to children and to those whom we consider our inferiors in education? Is this equivalent to the way we mute ourselves when talking to those who are lesser than ourselves, speaking in modulated and sweetened tone to children, slowly and with less vigour to the old, the lost, the needy? It is not simplicity of speech which calls forth the use of the verbal *up*, I think. English writers of children's books use it more frequently than American writers—at least among those whose books I analysed. Elmer Davis, speaking of weighty subjects with dignity and precision, uses it frequently. John Dewey uses it in writings which are far from simple—at any rate for this reader.

The conclusions I reached on the basis of my inquiry into the use of the verbal *up* are supported through my parallel inquiry into the *have to*. Briefly, the use of the *have to* also has been increasing, in fact more rapidly than that of the *up*. In *Jonathan Postfree*, an American play from

1807, it occurs once; in *Come Back Little Sheba*, 1949, it occurs over sixty times. A detailed study of its use as compared with the use of equivalent ways of relating the individual to his situation, indicates to me that this, like the *up*, is self-oriented, and is, to use an apparent paradox, to some extent spontaneous. The meaning of the *have to* ranges from the voluntary personal assumption of responsibility (I've got to do it, as equivalent to: it's up to me to do it) to the recognition of the personal application of a generic necessity; that is, of the translation of the *must* of environmental necessity, or the *ought to* of moral necessity to the *have to* of the personally chosen necessity, or personally assumed responsibility. The *have to* carries force. I have recorded the expressions: 'I *must* . . . but I am not going to'; 'I know I *should*, but I won't'; I *ought* to do my chemistry, but I *don't have to.*' The *have to* is the only 'compulsive' that leads surely to the act. When the Vassar students, whose after-dinner conversations were recorded over a period of two weeks, said 'I've got to' all but once before they left the group, they used the only phrasing of their situation which could express a force strong enough to move them to the sequel: 'and I'm going to'.

On the basis of the conclusion to which I was led through my study of the verbal *up* reinforced by the study of the *have to*, I would suggest that the question of the freedom of the self is of little or no concern here. If the rare occurrence of the terms *free* and *freedom* indicates small preoccupation with inner freedom, it may mean that freedom is irrelevant, or perhaps assumed and therefore out of mind. Or it may mean both of these. This conclusion would suggest that what is of concern, what is sought and prized is that which moves to the vigorous, the strong act. The participant in American culture then finds this motivation in the defining and stiffening limit. Free time does not motivate him to strong action, neither does the mere freedom to act. The schedule to which he has committed himself, the deadline he has assumed, the appointment he has made, these are the things which move him to act. Having taken the *must* as personal obligation or responsibility, it is up to him to carry it through.

In recent years, we have been impressed by the need for limits, because we believe that unlimited freedom is frightening. But to the American self, I do not know that the reaction to the unlimited 'I can' is necessarily one of fright. Rather, the unlimited freedom to, may mean a condition of inertia; and I think, one lacking in value. The linguistic clues discussed here, suggest the meaningful situation is the precise, delimited, defined situation; and it is this which calls forth the upsurge of spontaneity and strength.

Dorothy Lee

9

We often have difficulty in understanding a purely verbal notion. In *Alice in Wonderland* '. . . the patriotic archbishop of Canterbury found it advisable—'

'Found *what?*' said the Duck.

'Found *it*', the Mouse replied rather crossly: 'of course you know what "it" means.'

'I know what "it" means well enough when *I* find a thing' said the Duck: 'it's generally a frog, or a worm. The question is, what did the archbishop find?'

We feel happier when *it* is visible; then it's oriented in a way we understand. For in our workaday world, space is conceived in terms of that which separates visible objects. 'Empty space' suggests a field in which there is nothing *to see*. I will refer to a gasoline drum filled with pungent fumes or to a tundra swept by howling gales as 'empty' because nothing is visible in either case.

I do not believe that all cultures think this way. In one preliterate culture of which I have heard, the binding power of oral tradition is so strong that the eye is subservient to the ear. In the beginning was the Word, an auditory word, not the visual one of literate man. Idols are unknown;

instead, deities are depicted by dancers who *speak* and *sing*. Anthropologists visiting these people have occasionally been puzzled by the fact that though certain masks and other paraphernalia worn by the dancers appear almost identical, the natives clearly distinguish between them. They do this on the basis of the voices and songs associated with them. Moreover, the ocularly visible apparition is not nearly as common as the purely auditory one; perhaps *hearer* would be a better term than *seer* for their holy men.

In such a society, auditory orientation must play a very prominent role, one not lightly brushed aside, as it is with us. Of course, even we sometimes become aware of auditory space. Several years ago I had a temporary patch put over my left eye and in driving home became acutely conscious, purely on auditory grounds, of cars moving up from behind to pass me. My impairment had not improved my auditory sensitivity; it had simply made me aware of an orientation hitherto unconscious.

Not all of this is personal. When a wife calls to her husband, 'Oh, John' , we know that he is at greater than arm's length from her, for our language provides tonal patterns for structuring space under certain circumstances. Singing itself is addressed, from a distance, to a group, which it unites: 'Let me be known only as the man who wrote the songs of my people.'

But generally in our society to be real a thing must be visible. Not since Aristotle assured his *readers* that the sense of sight was, 'above all others', the one to be trusted, have we accorded to sound a primary role. Most of our thinking is done in terms of *visual* models, even when an auditory one might prove more efficient. From the recondite academic 'field' of specialization to the commonplace 'I'm from Missouri—show me', our speech attests to the force of visual metaphor. 'Time' has been neatly rendered visual by the clock so we can *see* what time it is; truth is generally defined in terms of what can be proved by observation and measurement. Mysticism and intuition are bad words among scientists; we are embarrassed by Newton's revelations and grateful that it was Darwin, not Wallace, who championed the cause of evolution.

Now every normal person, regardless of culture, spends the greater part of his waking activity in a visual world of three dimensions. If he thinks about the matter at all, he is inclined to conclude that this is the way, the only way, the world is made. It is therefore worth recalling that the child must *learn* to see the world as we know it. At or shortly after birth, his eyes are as perfectly developed a camera mechanism as they will ever be. In a sense they are too perfect and too mechanical, since they present him with a world in which everything is inverted, double, laterally reversed, and devoid of depth. In the course of time, by a tremendous tour de force of learning, he turns the world right side up, achieves binocular fusion, and reverses the lateral field so that he now sees his father as one person, erect, whole, and bilaterally oriented.

At the same time his growing capacity for movement leads him to explore this visual panorama tactually and kinaesthetically. This activity is the basis of the development of the dominant characteristic of visual experience: depth. Without motor movement and its attendant kinaesthesis, it is hard, if not impossible, to believe that depth perception would develop at all. Imagine a child incapable of motion from birth: that child would live in the two dimensional world of its own retinae. No identifiable person or object, as such, could emerge for him, since as his mother approached, she would appear as several different people of progressively greater size. Nor could such a child develop an awareness of himself. Even the congenitally blind child is not as handicapped: he has auditory space in which to function unimpaired by the hopeless visual conflicts of the hypothetical child and, more importantly, he can explore this auditory world tactually while in motion. In other words, the chief characteristic of visual space—depth—is not primarily derived from visual experience at all, but comes rather from locomotion and its attendant kinaesthesis.

We suppress or ignore much of the world as visually given in order to locate and identify *objects* in three dimensions. It is the objects which compel our attention and orient our behaviour; space becomes merely that which must be traversed in getting to or from them. It exists between them, but they define it. Without them you have empty space. Most people feel an obscure gratitude to Einstein because he is said to have demonstrated that 'infinite' space has a boundary of some kind. The gratitude flows, not because anyone understands how this can be, but because it restores to visual space one of its essential elements.

The essential feature of sound, however, is not that it be located at a point, but that it *be*, that it fill auditory space. We say 'the night shall be *filled* with music', just as the air is filled with fragrance; in both, locality is irrelevant. No one worries about where a loudspeaker is located; it can be any place that permits good listening. The concert-goer may even close his eyes to avoid distraction.

Auditory space has no point of favoured focus. It is a sphere without fixed boundaries with ourselves in the centre; Milton's—

a dark illimitable ocean,
without bound, without dimension, where length, breadth and height
And Time and place are lost.

We hear equally well from right or left, front or back, above or below. If we lie down, it makes no difference, whereas in visual space, the entire spectacle is altered. We can shut out the visual field by simply closing our eyes, but we are always triggered to respond to sound.

Audition has boundaries only in terms of upper and lower thresholds. We hear waves produced by double vibration cycles of about 16 cycles per second up to about 20,000 per second. The amount of energy needed to produce an auditory sensation is so small that, were the ears just slightly more sensitive, we could hear molecules of air crashing into each other, provided, of course, we could learn to ignore the continuous Niagara of sound such ears would detect in the circulation of blood!

Auditory space has no boundaries in the visual sense. The distance a sound can be heard is dictated more by its intensity than by the capacity of the ear. We might compare this to looking at a star, where visual sensation, transcending the vanishing point, is achieved, but at the sacrifice of the precise framework we call visual space. There is nothing in auditory space corresponding to the vanishing point in visual perspective. One can, with practice, learn to locate many objects by sound, but this can be done so much better by vision that few of us bother. We continue to be amazed at the 'psychic' powers of the blind who establish direction and orientation by translating auditory-tactual clues into the visual knowledge they once had, an orientation infinitely more difficult for the congenitally blind.

In general, auditory space lacks the precision of visual orientation. It is easy, of course, to determine whether a sound comes from the right or left, because the width of the head makes it inevitable that the ears be stimulated by slightly different phases of the wave (a difference of 16/10,000 of a second can be detected). But it is impossible, while blindfolded, to judge accurately whether a neutral buzzer, at a constant distance, is directly before or behind one, and similarly, whether directly overhead or underfoot.

The universe is the potential map of auditory space. We are not Argus-eyed, but we are Argus-eared. We hear instantly anything from any direction and at any distance, within very wide limits. Our first response to such sensation is to move head and body to train our eyes on the source of the sound. Thus the two sense avenues coordinate as a team, each supplying an essential element for survival which the other lacks.

Whereas the eyes are bounded, directed, and limited to considerably less than half the visible world at any given moment, the ears are all encompassing, constantly alert to any sound originating in their boundless sphere.

The ear is closely affiliated with man's emotional life, originally in terms of survival. The 'sudden loud sound' which Watson thought produced an instinctive (unlearned) fear response in the infant, still compels our quick (conditioned) fear response when perceived as, say, an automobile horn. It's the ambulance siren, not the blinker, which first warns us. Of what use would it be for a taxi driver to wave a flag or resort to any other visual equivalent for a warning? The onrushing cab itself is sufficient warning—if you happen to be looking that way! The dimensionless space of auditory sensation is the only hope in this circumstance; precisely because it is directionless, any sudden sound, from any quarter, will be attended to instantly.

Not all sounds are sudden and not all are fear-producing. Auditory space has the capacity to elicit the gamut of emotions from us, from the marching song to opera. It can be filled with sound which has no 'object', such as the eye demands. It need not be representational, but can speak, as it were, directly to emotion. Music can, of course, be visually evocative, as program music is, or it can be made to subserve the ends of visual presentation, as in the case of Tin Pan Alley tunes invented or stolen to fit lyrics. But there is no demand that music do either.

Poets have long used the word as incantation, evoking the visual image by magical acoustic stress. Preliterate man was conscious of this power of the auditory to make present the absent thing. Writing annulled this magic because it was a rival magical means of making present the absent sound. Radio restored it. In fact, in evoking the visual image radio is sometimes more effective than sight itself. The squeaking door in *Inner Sanctum* is far more terrifying over radio than that same door seen and heard on television, because the visual image that sound evokes comes from the imagination.

This interplay between sense perceptions creates a redundancy where, even if one element of a pattern is omitted, it is nevertheless inferred. We feel, hear, and see 'flaming, crackling red'; leave out 'red'—*it's still there*; green neither flames nor crackles. In *The Eve of St. Agnes*, Keats describes how objects feel, taste, sound, and smell:

> . . . her vespers done,
> Of all its wreathèd pearls her hair she frees;
> Unclasps her warmèd jewels one by one;

Loosens her fragrant bodice; by degrees
Her rich attire creeps rustling to her knees . . .

Elsewhere he describes fruit in terms of smell, taste, touch, even sound, and thus we experience the fruit; he uses lots of l's and o's and u's; the mouth drips with honey as it forms these sounds.

This sort of interplay creates a dynamic process—being, alive, the ritual drama—particularly in primitive societies where the association of elements in such patterns is especially strong.

Much of the intellectual excitement of 5th century Athens related to the discovery of the visual world and the translation of oral tradition into written and visual modes (probably the new role of the eye was as exciting to the Greeks as television is to us). The medieval world tried to channel the acoustic via Gregorian and liturgical chants, but it expanded into the visual world and the resulting bulge or usurpation probably had much to do with the creation of 'perspective' painting. For pure visual space is flat, about 180°, while pure acoustic space is spherical. Perspective translated into visual terms the depths of acoustic space. The unscrambling of this mélange occurred via the photograph which freed painters to return to flat space. Today we are experiencing the emotional and intellectual jag resulting from the rapid translation of varied visual and auditory media into one another's modalities.

D. C. Williams

MUTATIONS

In a corridor I saw an arrow pointing a certain way, and I thought of how that now inoffensive symbol had once been a thing of iron, an indomitable and mortal projectile, which penetrated the flesh of men and lions, and darkened the sun at Thermopylae, and gave to Harald Sigurdson six feet of English soil forever.

Days later, someone showed me a photograph of a Magyar horseman; a cord in loops circled his mount's breast. I knew that this cord, this lasso which formerly had sailed through the air and held the bulls in the pasture-ground, was now nothing but the insolent gala wear of Sunday riding gear.

In the cemetery of the West I saw a Runic Cross, carved in red marble; the arms were curved and outspread—and surrounded by a circle. This curtailed and compressed cross was emblematic of the other one, the cross with free arms, which stood, in turn, for the gibbet on which a god had writhed, for that 'vile machine' reviled by Lucian of Samosata.

Cross, cord, and arrow, ancient contrivances of man, nowadays debased, or elevated, into symbols: I do not know why they should astonish me, when there is on earth no single thing oblivion does not overtake, or which memory does not alter, and when no one knows the images into which the future will translate all things.

Jorge Luis Borges

take it from me kiddo
believe me
my country, 'tis of

you, land of the Cluett
Shirt Boston Garter and Spearmint
Girl With The Wrigley Eyes (of you
land of the Arrow Ide
and Earl &
Wilson
Collars) of you i
sing: land of Abraham Lincoln and Lydia E. Pinkham,
land above all of Just Add Hot Water And Serve—
from every B. V. D.

let freedom ring

amen.   i do however protest, anent the un
-spontaneous and otherwise scented merde which
greets one (Everywhere Why) as divine poesy per
that and this radically defunct periodical.   i would

suggest that certain ideas gestures
rhymes, like Gillette Razor Blades
having been used and reused
to the mystical moment of dullness emphatically are
Not To Be Resharpened. (Case in point

if we are to believe these gently O sweetly
melancholy trillers amid the thrillers
these crepuscular violinists among my and your
skyscrapers—Helen & Cleopatra were Just Too Lovely,
The Snail's On The Thorn enter Morn and God's
In His andsoforth

do you get me?) according
to such supposedly indigenous
throstles Art is O World O Life
a formula: example, Turn Your Shirttails Into
Drawers and If It Isn't An Eastman It Isn't A
Kodak therefore my friends let
us now sing each and all fortissimo A-
mer
i

ca, I
love,
You.   And there're a
hun-dred-mil-lion-oth-ers, like
all of you successfully if
delicately gelded (or spaded)
gentlemen (and ladies)—pretty

littleliverpill-
hearted-Nujolneeding-There's-A-Reason
americans (who tensetendoned and with
upward vacant eyes, painfully
perpetually crouched, quivering, upon the
sternly allotted sandpile
—how silently
emit a tiny violetflavoured nuisance:Odor?

ono.
comes out like a ribbon lies flat on the brush

e. e. cummings

We like to play twenty questions with our words. Everything is in a box within a box within a box, and if it is in one box it cannot be in another box within the same series, though it can have its place in each of several series of boxes. Here, for example, is Pussy, my black cat:

First series: The biggest box is labelled *material object*. Inside that is the box labelled *living being*, and inside that, *animal*. Then we have *mammal, feline, domestic cat, short-haired*, and in the smallest box sits Pussy, unique and alone.

Second series: Blackness, black objects, objects imbued with black pig. mentation, black fur, a black-furred animal, a black-furred cat, Pussy.

Most things are placed in a certain box in each of several series. But every box is in some series. Nothing is without a box, or in an isolated box.

I have a sudden image of my friend Jack, standing in the middle of his room, which was lined with book-shelves. On one wall he had essays, on another fiction, on another, biography, on another, history. Jack was holding a copy of *Lettres de mon Moulin*, which is part fiction, part essays, part autobiography, part even history. Poor Jack! I do not think it was coincidence that shortly after that occasion he lost that book. We must lose a great many ideas because we have devised a system in which there is no place for them.

We do not mind things being in more than one classificatory system, but we do not like them being in no system at all. Thus, when a lady says, 'I want to introduce you to my husband and the father of my child', we are quite prepared to shake hands with only one man, but if she says merely, 'This is John Smith', we feel she should have given a little more information. Even on that much information, we have probably already classified John Smith as male, probably English and a commoner, and probably on terms of social equality with the lady.

In a language which does not have classificatory nouns, such as *mammal, profession,* ideas would have to be handled in quite a different way. Things would be at the same time more precise and more blurred than with us. I mean that, when a cat is regarded as a cat and not as a particular sort of mammal, it is more precise in that it stands out as a cat away from a background of indistinguished mammals, and more blurred in that, not being fixed in a hierarchy of mammals, it may be related quite freely to a house or a spirit or to any other idea in the thinker's world.

The unreality of our classificatory nouns, which we are accustomed to think of as concrete, is shown up when we try to visualise, for example, an animal. We have to choose some particular animal to visualise, and the harder we try to form an image, the further away we get from the true meaning of the word; we probably end up by visualising a brown horse with a white right foreleg.

Adjectives

In our society, the tendency, both in love and friendship, is to be attracted by qualities rather than persons. We like people not for what they are in themselves, but because they are beautiful or rich or amusing, so if they lose their looks or their money or their wit, we lose our interest in them.

Except for certain kinds of love, such as the feeling of a mother for a new baby or of lovers for each other in the early stages of courtship, love and friendship in our society are generally based on the qualities possessed by persons rather than on the persons themselves. Even mother-love quickly changes to approval based on the qualities of the child. The founder of a society in Kansas to help unmarried mothers writes that the chief concern of the girls is to keep knowledge of their plight from their mothers; they feel, rightly or wrongly, that their mothers' love is not of the sort that will persist in face of the child's 'disgraceful' behaviour. We have some approach to the primitive conception of love in the romantic love stories of our literature, stories of the 'Romeo and Juliet' type. An anonymous seventeenth-century poet tries to express the idea of love without consideration of qualities in the lines:—

> To doat upon me ever.
> So hast thou the same reason still
> And love me still but know not why;
> Keep therefore a true woman's eye,

(But he is still enough of a child of European society as to present not-having-a-reason as a reason for loving.)

A truer explanation of love in our society is given by the girl who said, 'I love John for what he *is*, not for what he *has*; for instance, he *is* the owner of a brand-new Cadillac. . . .' When we try to think of or describe a person, we can do so only in terms of the qualities of that person. John may be rich, clever, amusing, but, even to his mother, he is never 'just John'. It is even easier for us to imagine the qualities without the man; our abstract nouns are literally abstracted from the person or the thing to which they were originally attached; cleverness and beauty are derived from our vision of persons who are clever and beautiful. (In some primitive languages we find what appear to be abstract nouns, but these prove to be not abstract nouns in our sense of the term; they denote actual things. Thus goodness is conceived almost as a substance which may enter into things, not as we conceive it, a quality common to all good things.) Sometimes a child sees things in a 'primitive' way. A little boy, asked what he was going to be when he grew up, replied, astonished at the silliness of the question, 'Why, a man, of course.' But his elders can no longer imagine a man without the label of his profession or whatever other quality they happen to think most important at any particular moment. The only person we can think of purely as a person is ourself, and that not always.

The Trobriander on the other hand, can see a thing or a person as a whole and as distinct and unrelated to any other thing or person. This does not mean that he sees persons as all alike or is unaware of their qualities. Malinowski in *The Sexual Life of Savages* describes in some detail the physical qualities and skills which are regarded as desirable in a lover or a friend. But the person appears to the lover or the friend as a person, not as a collection of attributes.

Our way of thinking is revealed in our grammar. Every noun may be qualified by several adjectives, of which we have a tremendous number, and in addition almost any other part of speech may be pressed into service as an adjective. We cannot describe anything accurately without adjectives. A potato may be raw or cooked, large or small, under- or over-ripe or have any of an infinite number of qualities. But the Trobriander does not so describe a yam; he has distinct, not even similar words for a ripe yam, a spotted yam, etc., and no doubt thinks of them as quite different things. We have something of the same use of language in technical fields; the sheep farmer differentiates between tegs, wethers, ewes, rams, etc. instead of using the word 'sheep' qualified by adjectives—but the word 'sheep' does exist and the more specialised terms are not in general use by laymen. Swahili is similar to the Trobriand language in this respect. There are only a few adjectives, many of which are fairly recent borrowings from Arabic. Of course an English-Swahili dictionary gives equivalents for many English adjectives, but these are only decapitated bodies of words; they are not functioning words until they have been equipped with a prefix which varies according to the class (the classification is primarily one of meaning) of the noun with which they are to be used. Normally other constructions are preferred to the noun-adjective combination. Thus, 'a just man' is 'mtu wa hati'—a man of justice. ('Mtu' means a person of either sex, a person considered without any attributes.) 'A wealthy person' is 'mwenye mali'—'mw-' personal concordal prefix, '-enye', having, 'mali', wealth. Thus the wealth is not inseparably linked with the person; in fact two different constructions may be used according as the wealth is considered to be permanently or temporarily attached to the person.

When we think of a person with his qualities firmly bound up with him, we think not only of the nature of his qualities but of the quantity of them. Not only is John rich or clever, but he is more or less rich or clever than other people. The Trobriand language has no simple way of expressing comparisons, for the Trobriander is not in the habit of comparing things. To him a thing is itself, seen neither as a compound of various factors nor as a factor in a larger compound. So when he feels

22

an emotion towards a person, he conceives only the person, not a collection of qualities.

Almost the only vestige which remains in our society of this way of looking at a person is the phenomenon of falling in love. But this does not fit in with our habits of thought. We appoint marriage counsellors who tell us to ignore this phenomenon as far as we can; thus we are eager to destroy our last traces of primitive good sense.

The Verb 'to be'

The verb 'to be' is used in English with several distinct meanings:

Simple equivalence or definition:
> The object in my hand is a pencil.
> A man is an adult male human being.

In this sense the verb is tautological. It is omitted in many languages, for example, Hebrew and Swahili.

Existence:
> I think, therefore I am.
> And God said unto Moses, I am that I am.

Here the philosophical concept of existence is introduced. In a truly monotheistic religion, it is the only attribute of the god. I do not think that some primitive peoples conceive of existence in this way. Our philosophers are much occupied with the question, and, with the essential polarity of our thought, it leads them to try to conceive non-existence. They do this by a sort of conjuring trick. I imagine a vase on the table. Now I imagine it gone. Now I have the idea of the non-existence of the vase. But could I imagine its non-existence if I had not imagined its existence in the first place? The mass of metaphysics based on this question is founded solely on the extension of the 'exist' meaning of the verb 'to be' from a particular object in a particular place at a particular time to cover the whole world of thought in infinite space and time. It seems to me an uncomfortable and unprofitable way of thinking. In Swahili there are two ways of saying 'There are no knives in the box.' One way emphasizes the absence of the knives, the other stresses the fact that they are not in the box, though they may be in some other place. But in neither case is the grammatical construction any sort of a verb 'to be'; it is a 'place suffix' or an 'indefinite place suffix' attached to the concordial prefix of the word for 'knives'. The knives are regarded as being absent in general, or absent from some particular place. I do not think there is any simple way of expressing the absolute non-existence of knives.

Inclusion of a smaller class in a larger one:
  A pig is a mammal.
  Toronto is a city.
In many European languages, this use of the verb 'to be' is confused with definition—*i.e.*, people do not distinguish the use in 'Toronto is a city' from the use in 'Toronto is a city on the north shore of Lake Ontario, latitude 44, longitude 79.' Not all languages are pre-occupied with arranging things in a diminishing series of classes that fit into each other like the boxes in a Chinese puzzle. Some omit the verb 'to be' in this sense as in the sense of definition.

Denotion of position in space at a given time:
  My wife is in the kitchen.
I think English is almost unique in using the verb 'to be' so freely in this sense. German uses 'sich finden', 'stehen', 'liegen' or any of several other verbs according to the precise meaning. French, too, uses a variety of verbs, such as 'se trouver', 'demeurer'. Italian distinguishes between a permanent and a temporary sojourn. In the example given, Italian would use 'stare' unless the speaker meant that he never allowed his wife out of the kitchen; the verb 'to be' is used for permanent position, as in 'Rome is in Italy.'

Attribution of a quality to a thing:
  The book is red.
This construction is found in many European languages, though here again the verb is tautological, especially when, as in French, Italian and many other languages, a morphological modification clearly shows that the adjective belongs to the noun. Latin in particular strongly relies on morphology for this purpose. The position of an adjective in a sentence is determined by considerations of emphasis, harmony and, in verse, prosody; it may be far from the noun to which it relates, its grammatical ending being regarded as sufficient anchorage.

German makes an interesting distinction. In the phrase 'the red book', the adjective has to agree with the noun in number, gender and case, but when the adjective is used attributively, as in 'The book is red', it has a neuter form, thus asserting, so to speak, its independence.

The Possessive
English uses the possessive very vaguely and very extensively. It fails to distinguish between the closest and the loosest forms of possession; even things essentially unpossessable are attributed to owners.

Some primitive peoples make very clear linguistic distinctions between different forms of possession. Trobriand has different possessive forms for 'my blood' (part of me) and 'my house' (belonging to me). Wintu does not use the possessive for either parts of the body or clothes, as long as they continue to be part of the person; but a possessive form is used for cut-off hair or cast-off garments. French makes something of the same sort of distinction in that the possessive is not used for parts of the body (except occasionally to avoid ambiguity), but is used for articles of clothing.

An Italian distinction is also interesting. In general, the definite article is required before a possessive, but the article is omitted in the singular when referring to a family relation, e.g., 'la mia casa', but 'mia figlia'.

The English use of the possessive in the phrase 'the king's person' is, I think, very significant. The body is regarded as separate from the ego, but owned by it, as a man might own a horse. Christian, and particularly Protestant philosophy, is closely bound up with this uncomfortable relationship.

Casting the net of possession still further, the charwoman says, 'Don't walk on my clean floor!' She does not mean that the floor belongs to her, or even that its cleanness belongs to her, but that she has a certain connection with the cleanness which gives her the right to insist on its preservation.

By our use of the possessive pronoun, we lay claim to things which are indisputably not private property. I remember as a young child being told to recite 'my' three times table. I realised that by learning the three times table I had somehow made it mine in the sense that it did not belong in the same way to a child who had not learned it. But it was not mine if it could also belong to anybody who took the trouble to learn it. The fact that it was not really mine was borne in on me when I found that any attempt to modify it on the grounds that I could do what I like with my own property met with a poor reception. It is significant that I felt that a thing could not be mine and somebody else's at the same time; the idea of common property is difficult to instil into a child in our society.

The morphology of the possessive adjective may lay stress on the possessor, the thing possessed or on both equally. Thus in German the possessive adjective agrees in gender and number with both the possessor and the thing possessed. In English it agrees with the former only, in French, (except in number) with the latter only.

Joan Rayfield

The CITY no longer exists, except as a cultural ghost for tourists. Any highway eatery with its tv set, newspaper, and magazine is as cosmopolitan as New York or Paris.

The PEASANT was always a suburban parasite. The farmer no longer exists; today he is a 'city' man.

The METROPOLIS today is a classroom; the ads are its teachers. The classroom is an obsolete detention home, a feudal dungeon.

The metropolis is OBSOLETE. Ask the Army.

The INSTANTANEOUS global coverage of radio-tv makes the city form meaningless, functionless. Cities were once related to the realities of production and inter-communication. Not now.

Until WRITING was invented, we lived in acoustic space, where the Eskimo now lives: boundless, directionless, horizonless, the dark of the mind, the world of emotion, primorial intuition, terror. Speech is a social chart of this dark bog.

SPEECH structures the abyss of mental and acoustic space, shrouding the race; it is a cosmic, invisible architecture of the human dark. Speak that I may see you.

WRITING turned a spotlight on the high, dim Sierras of speech; writing was the visualization of acoustic space. It lit up the dark.

These five kings did a king to death.

A goose's quill put an end to talk, abolished mystery, gave architecture and towns, brought roads and armies, bureaucracies. It was the basic metaphor with which the cycle of CIVILIZATION began, the step from the dark into the light of the mind. The hand that filled a paper built a city.

The handwriting is on the celluloid walls of Hollywood; the Age of Writing has passed. We must invent a NEW METAPHOR, restructure our thoughts and feelings. The new media are not bridges between man and nature: they are nature.

The MECHANIZATION of writing mechanized the visual-acoustic metaphor on which all civilization rests; it created the classroom and mass education, the modern press and telegraph. It was the original assembly-line.

Gutenberg made all history SIMULTANEOUS: the transportable book brought the world of the dead into the space of the gentleman's library; the telegraph brought the entire world of the living to the workman's breakfast table.

PHOTOGRAPHY was the mechanization of the perspective painting and of the arrested eye; it broke the barriers of the nationalist, vernacular space created by printing. Printing upset the balance of oral and written speech; photography upset the balance of ear and eye.

Telephone, gramophone, and RADIO are the mechanization of post-literate acoustic space. Radio returns us to the dark of the mind, to the invasions from Mars and Orson Welles; it mechanizes the well of loneliness that is acoustic space: the human heart-throb put on a PA system provides a well of loneliness in which anyone can drown.

Movies and TV complete the cycle of mechanization of the human sensorium. With the omnipresent ear and the moving eye, we have abolished writing, the specialized acoustic-visual metaphor which established the dynamics of Western civilization.

By surpassing writing, we have regained our WHOLENESS, not on a national or cultural but cosmic plane. We have evoked a super-civilized sub-primitive man.

NOBODY yet knows the language inherent in the new technological culture; we are all deaf-blind mutes in terms of the new situation. Our most impressive words and thoughts betray us by referring to the previously existent, not to the present.

We are back in acoustic space. We begin again to structure the primordial feelings and emotions from which 3000 years of literacy divorced us.

Hands have no tears to flow   ⁳

DYLAN THOMAS

I met Dylan Thomas yesterday—that doesn't mean I rushed up and told him how wonderful he was; it means that I sat three feet away from him in the Union lounge while Professor Brewster Ghiselin and his following questioned him for an hour and a half. Throughout it all you could feel the relationship between Dylan Thomas and Ghiselin—tremendous respect on both sides, and yet too great a distance ever to be close. Both of them shy men, really, who have hung their souls out on the line, yet kept firmly established egos: Ghiselin, the scholar-poet and host, never quite sure that his man wouldn't· get up and leave through the open window; and Thomas, out of place, uneasy at being exposed on all sides, yet on his best behaviour, sticking it out.

Ghiselin led off with a brief introduction and then asked why a poet went around on a reading tour. Thomas, looking down at the table, facing no one, said softly: 'My God, that's a hard question. I'm afraid I shall have to answer it straight: it's a way of seeing the country and I haven't any money. It's a matter of ego as well.'

Ghiselin: But why is the poetry read aloud? Does it aid understanding?

Thomas: People come to have a look at me. Here's a little fat man come to make a fool of himself, they think, and since they don't listen to what I read, it doen't matter whether I make sense or not. . . . But that isn't quite fair of me—I am enjoying myself.

Ghiselin: You read much on the B.B.C. Do you feel that poetry must be read aloud before it is complete? Does it bring you closer to the meaning?

Thomas: Yes—perhaps it helps in the interpretation or emphasis. It brings you closer to the poet.

Question from a student: Do you listen to the sound of your own words? Is that as important to you as the rhyme and metre?

Thomas: Oh, God, that's a hard one too. Yes—you can struggle with rhyme and metre and style and still not have a poem. I'm sorry I'm not answering the way you would like.

Student: But why do you read your own poetry?

Thomas: For the noise it makes. And for the memory of the experience of writing it. But it has already said everything it had to say.

Student: Do you say the words aloud as you write them?

Thomas: Yes. That's why I live in a hut on a cliff.

Another student: Is it necessary for a poem to have an outcome? Robert Frost says that a poem should be resolved. It should not be too obscure to be understood. I have difficulty in understanding you, especially your early sonnets.

Thomas: Then you should read Robert Frost. . . . But you are right: to the poet, at least, there is always an outcome. Those sonnets are only the writings of a boily boy in love with shapes and shadows on his pillow.

Ghiselin: I've wondered about the sonnets. I could never see anything very deep in them. It's good to know I need search no further.

Thomas: Well, they would be of interest to another boily boy. Or a boily girl. (Long pause.) Boily-girly.

Here Thomas laughed to himself and seemed lost in very amusing word combinations—while everyone sat petrified, until somebody brought him back to us: Is it ever fair deliberately to confuse the reader?

Thomas: I thought someone would take me up on that. No—it is a deliberate avowal of your own inefficiency. It is impossible to be too clear. You can state too bluntly all you know, or put down very clearly what you intend, which may be very narrow and even cruel. But we don't know about anything. Especially people, nobody knows. There are scientific terms, but—why doesn't the water fly out of the ocean when the earth whirls? Because it is a ball of magic. It is impossible to be too clear. I am trying for more clarity now. At first I thought it enough to leave an impression of sound and feeling and let the meaning seep in later, but since I've been giving these broadcasts and reading other men's poetry as well as my own, I find it better to have more meaning at first reading.

Ghiselin: But, on the other hand, isn't it possible to narrow and fix a meaning to the exclusion of richer levels of meaning?

Thomas: Oh God, isn't an education wonderful!

Ghiselin: I shall be silent from now on.

Thomas: No, I mean it as a compliment. You say things so well, and I'm ashamed to be flippant and go down the side alleys. . . .

Student: Do you find it necessary to study other things in order to find increasing satisfaction in your own poetry?

Thomas: There is never any satisfaction—that's why I write another poem. Do I study other things? Yes, people. . . . (Long pause, the questioner nodding thoughtfully), then: Me!

Another student: Why do you write poetry, Mr. Thomas?

Thomas: Because I have the time. Because I have to live too; (mumbled) I don't know why. . . . It is very slow work, however. Only five poems published in the last six years. It is slow, but sometimes there is just nothing better to do. Sometimes it feels very good to have a blank piece of paper in front of you, and you put down the first line. Then you look at all the paper and think, Now I've got to rhyme this. And it's work! Oh God, it's awful! . . . I write some very bad poems.

Student: What happens to them?

Thomas: I keep them—too much of an egoist to throw them away. But neither do I do as Rossetti did, who buried them with his wife and had to dig them up later. I keep them in a drawer.

Student: What do you do with them?

Thomas: Nothing. When it's written it's finished.

Ghiselin: Perhaps you don't read your old poems over because there is a chance you might become infatuated with them and continue to write the same poem over and over. Some poets do.

Thomas: Jove! I never thought of that! I wonder what's in the drawer. (Pantomime.) This isn't so bad after all! Delightful! (He was gone again.)

Student: Who decides whether your poems are good or bad?

Thomas: I do. Nobody reads the bad ones.

Student: Then you don't ask a publisher for an opinion?

Thomas: Oh, no. If he didn't like one that I thought was good, it would be too terrible.

Student: If your own poetry gives you no satisfaction, is there any which does?

Thomas: That's easy: Shakespeare!

Student: Who is the best of the moderns?

Thomas: The nice thing about poetry is that it isn't a competitive field. There isn't any *best;* but I do like Thomas Hardy, D. H. Lawrence, W. H. Auden and——(Here, Dr.——on my left squealed in surprise, and I missed the fourth name.)

Student: How do you tell whether a poem is good or not?

Thomas: If I like it.

Student: But what do you go by?

Thomas: I like one because it is better than the others. (Silence.) Before I find a poem I like I have to pass over a great many that I don't like. When I find one I like, I read it. I don't know why. The big problem is to find the poem, then read it—hang by your ears from the chandeliers, or however you read poetry—and enjoy it.

Ghiselin: Perhaps we should do as you suggest and like a poem because we think it better than others, but students have to pull it apart and analyse why they like it and write it all down for a professor.

Thomas: People who think they know T. S. Eliot find it unbelievable that he enjoys Kipling, that rowdy rhymster. That is, the people who think they know Kipling too. Some of his poetry is excellent. (Very long pause. Dylan Thomas sips at his glass of water like a kitten bobbing its nose in a saucer. The glass is still full at the end of the session after at least a dozen embarrassed sips.)

Student: Do you address your noise only to yourself?

Thomas: Oh no. No. Yes—well, I *am* lots of people. I think I am lots of people at any rate. Of course, I know, and the birds know, I'm only a fat little fool ranting on a cliff, but it seems that I am lots of people.

Young lady: Has your style changed?

Thomas: Style? Yes. No—I'm still after the same things if that's what you mean.

Ghiselin: Your poetry seems to open little doors in quite ordinary and common events, sometimes by only shifting an image slightly to one side to let in the new idea.

Thomas: How nicely you say it! That is exactly what I would like my poetry to do some day.

Lady: Do you revise?

Thomas: No, I work it out a phrase at a time. It is very slow, but when it is once finished, all the revision has been done, and I don't change it.

Lady: Then it may take several days?

Thomas: Months. Years. It might never be finished. But I am a patient man.

Ghiselin: You always seem to put in your poetry just what you are seeing at the moment—the heron, and the birds near the estuary, for instance?

Thomas: Yes—yes. I wanted to write about the cliff, and there was a crow flying above it, and that seemed a good place to begin, so I wrote about the crow. Yes, if I see a bird, I put it in whether it belongs or not.

Ghiselin: Do you leave it there?

Thomas: If it is happy and at home in the poetry I do. But really I should get a blind for my window.

Student: But you do have some idea of what you are going to say?

Thomas: Sometimes. You don't just sit and wait for the little doors to open. Twenty years ago I would have said 'inspiration'. It's hard work. But sometimes the mood is enough. Say a poet is gay and he wants to write a gay poem—about anything. It is spring, or he has a new pair of shoes, or his wife has left him. Everything is gaiety. But then, suddenly, in the middle of the poem, he might miss his wife. It would be a very sad poem. You can't always follow your original plan.

Another student: Do you pay any attention to critics,——, for instance?

Thomas: Yes. Sometimes I wake up in the night and wonder about them. I don't know what they have against me. As far as——goes, it is a personal matter I'm sure. He just can't abide me. He can't stand to read me at all. I don't know why. I pay attention to the praise too—it's easier to take, although it isn't any truer and I don't believe it any more than the other. I mean, I can't be bought with a few sentences. I don't think they will change me. I know what kind of a man I am. (Quietly.) Thirty-seven years with the same head. . . .

And so it went on, until Ghiselin asked Thomas to read one of his poems. He arose for the first time, gathered up his five books and stuffed them in his briefcase. I thought he was offended, but he finished stowing them away, kept one out, and turned back to us: 'I brought all these books in case I would be too frightened to answer your questions. I haven't answered them, but I wasn't frightened. Thank you for asking me'.

He smiled and sat down again, and began to talk in a soft voice about his father, who, he said, had been a militant atheist, whose atheism had nothing to do with whether there was a god or not, but was a violent and personal dislike for God. He would glare out of the window and growl: 'It's raining, blast Him!' or, 'The sun is shining—Lord, what foolishness!' He went blind and was very ill before he died. He was in his eighties, and he grew soft and gentle at the last. Thomas hadn't wanted him to change. . . .

And all at once the little poet began to read, and his voice raged and surged with power and anger and a terrible desolation. He read 'Do not go gentle into that good night'. It was slow and rhythmic and deep. His eyes were bent down on the book, but he was not reading, for they would remain fixed for a long time and then wander over both pages for a moment and then freeze again. I can't express how startling the change was in him, from the shy, humble, apologetic, patiently eager man, to this tidal wave of humanity. I was uneasy at first because I felt that in either one position or the other he was only acting, but I could find no trace of insincerity ever. I suppose he knows best. He is lots of people.

Marjorie Adix

Dylan Thomas was born in Swansea in 1914; he died in New York in 1953. He is a voice of the age of trial and transformation. The title of his last volume of verse is itself an emblem of these times (and it comes, as we might expect, from Donne): *Deaths and Entrances*. The literature of the nineteenth century seems middle-aged (and the Nineties and Edwardians a second childhood), belongs to a plateau of process and development. We are back in the valleys and scrambling up the escarpments. Our private lives are formed by the inquiry into childhood; our politics is the arithmetic of survival. We exist at the boundaries of life, and our poet should be a bard of dawns and graves, of deaths and entrances. And such was he.

He came upon us from the outside. Not from the universities, where the poet is a living dog, or from the cities, where he is a dead lion. Dylan Thomas's landscape was as primitive as that of a frog, or any amphibian. Shore, mud, hill, trees, wind, birds, foxes, man. All his world is on a slant, from water to fire of the sun, down to the deep and up to the sky. 'Man be my metaphor', he said. And man's blood is salt like the sea, while man's mind is full of spaces like the spaces between the stars. On the boundary between sea and stars, between blood and mind, this strange bard erected his imagination, in which fire and water, destruction and desire, are the poles of human experience.

We needed someone who had not had time to form a style from among the styles of the period *entre deux guerres,* who would make a clean start. The new starts are always old too. Nothing is new; the new is a rebirth, a transformation. Eliot, for example, recalled the Augustinian divided man of Thomas Browne, dwelling in divided and distinguished worlds, whose orb of flesh beholds not felicity, whose salvation is a stair, a ladder leading into the heart of a rose. At the bottom of the stair, where we breathe and move, the spiral flattens into a hopeless round, symbolized by the Circle Line of the London tube, by the future prophesied for Edward and Lavinia in *The Cocktail Party,* by the dead accents of the dead voices in *Sweeney Agonistes:*

> Nothing to see but the palmtrees one way
> And the sea the other way,
> Nothing to hear but the sound of the surf.
> Nothing at all but three things
> > What things?
> Birth, copulation and death.

But Dylan Thomas went further back, over the edge of the waste land, past Hamlet's graveyard, to the primitive anthropomorphic vision of the bards and the Bible, for whom the world is man's body. In the very years when the human body was a statistical unit, either for the dole or the pension plan, a subject for the study of antibiotics in humane hospitals or of basic reflexes in concentration camps, he announced, at first wildly, then by times majestically, that the body is everything— including God—that it is simply all a poet can know and all he needs to know. And that was what we needed, and still need to hear, that to kill a man's body is to kill the world.

But perhaps, in the poetry of Dylan Thomas, it is man's body with the head cut off. What, for example, are we to make of a poem that begins like this:

> Because the pleasure-bird whistles after the hot wires
> Shall the blind horse sing sweeter?
> Convenient bird and beast lie lodged to suffer
> The supper and knives of a mood.

Reading Hardy's 'The Blinded Bird' does not help much. The common reader will content himself with calculating how many beers it takes to make a poem like that. And for those who expect, indeed welcome difficulties in a poem, especially a twentieth-century poem, but expect the difficulties to be capable of solution through the encyclopedia or memorization of a set of private references, such poems as this one are like an insult, a belch in the drawing room, a madman in the library. 'Romance without reason', says one critic, 'inhuman and glandular.'

But consider Thomas's own description of his kind of composition: 'A poem by myself needs a host of images, because its centre is a host of images. I make one image—though "make" is not the word, I let, perhaps, an image be "made" emotionally in me and then apply to it what intellectual and critical forces I possess—, let it breed another, let that image contradict the first, make, of the third image bred out of the other two together, a fourth contradictory image.'

How mixed up this is (or seems), how delightfully unhelpful, how garrulous! But there is something there; he is outlining the ambivalent process perfectly described in a line from one of his poems:

The dear daft time I take to nudge the sentence.

This is not the reduction of poetic creation to 'unconscious impulse' or the 'perpetual flow of irrational thought in the form of images', slogans of the New Apocalypse poets of the thirties who took him as their Shelley and Sir Herbert Read as their Coleridge. We are told that of late he spent more and more time over his poems, fashioning them with lapidary care. 'I work it out a phrase at a time', he said. 'It is very slow. . . . But I am a patient man.'

We must conclude that Thomas, being a greater poet than any self-confessed irrationalist, raised for himself questions of composition which transcend the naive simplistic formulations of the avant-garde artists, wet behind the ears from Freud, or any manifesto of neo-romanticist cliques. And by his accomplishment, even without his comment upon it, he invites us to think about the element of the irrational in artistic creation, explored from Plato (in *Ion*) to T. S. Eliot. Here he makes a poetic statement of the problem:

And from the first declension of the flesh
I learnt man's tongue, to twist the shapes of thoughts
Into the stony idiom of the brain,
To shade and knit anew the patch of words
Left by the dead, who in their moonless acre,
Need no word's warmth. . . .
I learnt the verbs of will, and had my secret;
The code of night tapped on my tongue;
What had been one was many sounding minded.
('From love's first fever')

'The code of night tapped on my tongue' is a good Platonic statement; it is an image of the artistic process conceived of as mysterious *making*. The shapes that emerge from the psychic underground, the womb and tomb of mind (which is the womb and tomb of the gods and muses), these are the stuff of which poetry is shaped. The writing of a poem is a discovery, but paradoxically a discovery in a well-known country, the country of words, mapped by syntax and conventional idiom. One critic, defining Thomas's kind of poetry, says that 'the poet conventionally offers what he knows he has found, but Thomas offers the process of discovery itself.' This is, I take it, just about the antithesis of: 'What oft was thought, but ne'er so well expressed.' More like, some might say, 'What ne'er was thought, and oft so ill expressed.'

And certainly it is true that when this foray into language is carried to frenetic extremities, poetry becomes the madhouse of language, or at best just handsome noise, what Thomas himself called 'the lovely gift of the gab'. Outrageous puns ('each minstrel angle') and gnomic derangements ('quickness of hand in the velvet glove'; 'once below a time'; 'my camel's eye will needle through the shroud') turn Thomas's poems into a linguistic kaleidoscope.

It is possible to read him for this, and this only, astonished by the rocketing language, occasionally compelled to admiration by the verbal cleverness. One gets as much of Eliot by making a list of his sources, or of Hopkins by counting his syllables. There is more, and it arises from his sensual awareness of his body and his virtual annihilation of the distinction between perceiving subject and natural object perceived.

In his prose, both the autobiographical *Portrait of the Artist as a Young Dog* and the symbolic short pieces, what Blake would call 'memorable fancies', we might hope to surprise his images more diffusely set out than in the poems, as it were moving more slowly, easier to catch. So, in this matter of bodily awareness, there is an important passage in the *Portrait*:

> I felt all my young body like an excited animal surrounding me, the torn knees bent, the bumping heart, the long heat and depth between the legs, the sweat prickling in the hands, the tunnels down to the eardrums, the little balls of dirt between the toes, the eyes in the sockets, the tucked-up voice, the blood racing, the memory around and within flying, jumping, swimming and waiting to pounce. There, playing Indians in the evening, I was aware of me myself in the exact middle of a living story, and my body was my adventure and my name.

This is the self hidden in the sensual heart, peering at the world through the 'five and country senses'. In another passage we see the self at once united with and transforming the world. After the act of love, the boy dreams:

Out of love he came marching, head on high, through a cave between two doors to a vantage hall room, with a view above the earth. He walked to the last rail before pitch space; though the earth bowled round quickly, he saw every plough crease and beast's print, man track and water drop, comb, crest, and plume mark, dust and death groove and signature and time-cast shade, from ice field to ice field, sea rims to sea centres, all over the apple-shaped ball under the metal rails beyond the living doors. He saw through the black thumbprint of a man's city to the fossil thumb of a once lively man of meadows; through the grass and clover fossil of a country print to the whole hand of a forgotten city drowned under Europe; through the handprint to the arm of an empire broken like Venus; through the arm to the breast, from history to the thigh, through the thigh in the dark to the first and west print between the dark and the green Eden; and the garden was undrowned, to this minute and forever, under Asia in the earth that rolled on to its music in the beginning evening. When God was sleeping, he had climbed a ladder, and the room three jumps above the final rung was roofed and floored with the live pages of the book of days; the pages were gardens, the built words were trees, and Eden grew above him into Eden, and Eden grew down into Eden through the lower earth, an endless corridor of boughs and birds and leaves.

One is really embarrassed by the wealth of symbolic material in this passage, which in my opinion contains about the whole meaning of the poems in a swirling nebula of images. These occult sentences remind us of so many things: of those guided tours of the female body so delightfully conducted by the Elizabethan poets, of the dream-work as explored by Freud, of the book of Genesis. It may be possible, however, to make out a few of the elements clearly.

First, the ground of this sensibility is a self-consciousness for which the body is not an agent of intelligence but a living wise entity, and the end of speech is the statement of the wisdom of the body. Thomas apparently saw intuitively that apocalyptic imaginery is all anthropomorphic, that the world of beginnings and endings is in the shape of man's body. The whole occult tradition, from the Kabbala to Thomas, is a revelation of a vision geometrically comprehended by a cross in a circle, and naturalistically expounded in terms of the correspondences between the members of the human body and the parts of the universe, earthly and heavenly. Once one has opened his mind to these associations, the passage just quoted (to say nothing of the poems) begins to fall into its traditional setting, and one can see it as simultaneously psychology, history and religion, all centred upon the myth of Eden.

The emergence from the cave, the womb, signifies the emergence of man upon the earth, and human history is glanced at from its beginnings. Man has created his history by his hand, with its opposable thumb; the modern city, man's peculiar creation, the symbol of civilization, is a black thumb-print, succeeding the pastoral work of an earlier culture, succeeding the old cities remembered as Atlantis, the lost civilization, or by extension as Rome, the empire of Venus guide of Aeneas, symbolized by the broken arm of the Venus de Milo. But the lost world is mythically the Golden Age, or Eden, the 'undrowned' *i.e.*, antediluvian world 'under Asia'. Eden, in the analogy of the body, is the sex: the female sex, the garden; the male sex, the tree. Also, theologically, there are two Edens: the Eden above (which, since we are fallen, we can only peer into when God is sleeping—or when we spy from the tower of poetry), and the Eden below, the image of which lies beneath the fallen world, and is traced in what Sir Thomas Browne called 'hieroglyphicks' in the world of nature. The two Edens constitute the axis of the 'apple-shaped ball', the oblate spheroid of the earth. Also, since analogues are reversible, remember that Eden exists only by virtue of an *uneaten* apple. Finally, we might add that childhood is, if not the pure Eden state, at least the nearest we can reach to it through conscious memory; it lies beneath us as we totter on the Proustian stilts of our years.

Bearing these relationships in mind, let us look at the opening of 'Fern Hill':

> Now as I was young and easy under the apple boughs
> About the lilting house and happy as the grass was green,
>> The night above the dingle starry,
>> Time let me hail and climb
>> Golden in the heydey of his eyes,
> And honoured among waggons I was prince of the apple towns
> And once below a time I lordly had the trees and leaves
>> Trail with daisies and barley
>> Down the rivers of the windfall light.

This is one of Thomas's Songs of Innocence, for Eden is also Wales; Eden is where you were a child. 'It was all shining', he sings, 'it was Adam and maiden.' This is the apotheosis of pastoral.

The sea, the drowning place, is the place of beginnings, the woman, specifically the womb in which man lies, out of which his flesh emerges as land out of the sea, a re-enactment of Creation. (In Claudel's French, this identity is expressed as the pun on *mer* and *mère*.) Thomas is a poet of genesis—which makes him a poet of *Genesis*. Here is his own description of his imagination at work:

Water and fire, sea and apple-tree. He sharpened his pencil and shut the sky out, shook back his untidy hair, arranged the papers of a devilish story on his desk, and broke the pencil-point with a too-hard scribble of sea and fire on a clean page. . . . Under the eyelids, where the inward light drove backwards, through the skull's base, into the wide first world on the faraway eye, two love-trees smouldered like sisters.

And the poems are filled with the flaming landmarks he set up on his way to Eden.

But if Eden, as the place of genesis, is the womb, it is also the grave: our birth is dying. This traditional paradox Thomas expresses in terms of the

Incarnate devil in a talking snake,
The central plains of Asia in his garden,
In shaping-time the circle stung awake,
In shapes of sin forked out the bearded apple.

'There shall be serpents in your tides', he says to woman. The snake twined about the tree is a phallic image, indeed the Fall may be seen as a violation of Eve's innocence. The unabashed sexual image in the lines just quoted suggests this, and it is explicit in his reference elsewhere to 'the tree-tailed worm that mounted Eve', which might serve as a provocative caption for Blake's illustration of the temptation in *Paradise Lost*. The 'fathering worm' creates—and destroys.

Also the worm twined about the tree is a tower with a winding stair. In 'Prologue to an Adventure', which opens with a phrase reminiscent of the Bible and of Thomson's *City of Dreadful Night*, 'As I walked through the wilderness of this world, as I walked through the wilderness', the poet sees visions: 'Sideways the snake and the woman stroked a cross in the air'; he sees 'a woman confronted by a tower'; later he sees a drowned city. The tower is the complement of the sea; indeed we learn from this vision that it is a 'sea-tower'. Thomas, like the surrealists, was obsessed by the tower image, but he made something very brilliant out of it. He sits down to write:

The word is too much with us. He raised his pencil so that its shadow fell, a tower of wood and lead, on the clean paper; he fingered the pencil tower. . . . The tower fell, down fell the city of words, the walls of a

41

poem. . . . Image, all image, he cried to the fallen tower as the night came on, whose harp is the sea, whose burning candle is the sun?

What tower is a tower of words? Why, Babel, the place of noisy words, of the 'lovely gift of the gab', symbol of pride and death, also of the variety and impermanence of language. So he cries:

> Am I not all of you by the directed sea
> Where bird and shell are babbling in my tower?

The poet is himself a tower of Babel, echo of and spokesman for all the natural voices, from sea to sun, from water to fire:

> Shut, too, in a tower of words, I mark
> On the horizon walking like the trees
> The wordy shapes of women, and the rows
> Of the star-gestured children in the park.
> Some let me make you of the vowelled beeches,
> Some of the oaken voices, from the roots
> Of many a thorny shire tell you notes,
> Some let me make you of the water's speeches.
>   ('Especially when the October wind')

That poem is from his first published volume, when he was twenty. Time tracks you down, 'like a running grave'. 'I saw time murder me', he says in another poem. The devil of 'green Adam's cradle' is time,

> with his torch and hour-glass, like a sulphur priest,
> His beast-heel cleft in a sandal.

Time is the enemy of the flesh, the destroyer of the seasons. The murky images of death which inform the sensuality of Thomas's early poems arise from his identification of self with nature. He feels he should bear fruit like a vine, an apple-tree, but 'for three lean months in the bloody/ Belly of the rich year' he has written nothing. The sombre cycle which begins in green Eden is completed by the worm and winding sheet, the worm who intrudes upon the maiden innocence of life and poet. This is the theme of his best-known poem, the much anthologized 'The force that through the green fuse drives the flower.' Painfully, he discovered that Eden can be recovered through love. Still extravagant, his eloquence matured; the feverish images of the early poems are displaced by a new joy and power. 'I am trying for more clarity now', he said. In that year sacred to poets since Dante, he writes a 'Poem on his Birthday', 'His driftwood thirty-fifth wind turned age', by the shore where 'Herons, steeple-stemmed, bless', and 'counts [his] blessings aloud':

42

Four elements and five
Senses, and a man a spirit in love
Tangling through this spun slime
To his nimbus bell cool kingdom come
And the lost, moonshine domes,
And the sea that hides his secret selves
Deep in its black, base bones,
Lulling of spheres in the seashell flesh.

The poet comes out of suffering into light, and along his shore pace the druid herons, in his heart 'music of elements'. The sea is his Bible, he says in that fine poem 'Over Sir John's hill', open at a new place, 'at a passage/ Of psalms and shadows among the pincered sand-crabs dancing', and poetry is a sacramental record of life, a prayer:

I who hear the time of the slow
Wear-willow river, grave,
Before the lunge of the night, the notes on this time-shaken
Stone, for the sake of the souls of the slain birds sailing.

In these lines you can hear the change of tone from the earlier poems. It is not consistent; one cannot point to a date after which there is a difference, but it is there, and the roots of it were in his beginnings. As he put it himself, 'Thirty-seven years with the same head.'

The neo-romantic irrationality, of which young Thomas stood in danger, produces an art of despair, in which the poet is a hapless pedestrian caught in the two-way traffic between conscious and unconscious. In this 'inevitable conflict of images', as Thomes significantly termed it, each element contains its opposite, each act is balanced by its reaction, each symbol exists by virtue of its other-ness, and all is circular and self-destructive. Eden exists as innocence—and death; the tower rises—to fall. Ultimately the romantic can find a 'momentary peace' only in a narcissistic paralysis, where desire faces its own impossible reflection. (Thomas's first poems are filled with this image of the 'double'.) When the irrational becomes a cult, it is the most precisely ordered of all forms of existence, the most determined. It does not admit the miraculous or even the unexpected, for everything is in a sense miraculous and every-thing is expected.

Dylan Thomas began as prisoner of his own images, punished by his own imaginative dialectic. His love for nature (including his flesh, his 'naked fellow') was of that order described by Alcibiades in the *Symposium*, a desire to fuse the separate existences of lover and beloved, to make whole again that which has been split. His imagery and construction were hot and writhing because they represented his desperate attempt to make all things himself, which is the tempestuous counterpart of the contemplative's attempt to lose himself in all things, the perfect Pythagorean solution to the problem of existence. The result is a kind of poetic solipsism which dismays while it attracts, and poems full of sound and fury. Yet he did not end as a poetical machine, shouting his antithetic symbols down the insatiable maws of the more precious critics. He began to dream, out of the very sensual images which obsessed him, out of the Bible which is the only book he seems really to have *known*, a dream of transformation, of a miracle.

A dream of God, who turned out to be the body he had lived in all the time. The snake, the tree, the rod, the tower, the ark—all these are types of the incarnate God, who is the bodily statement of love, who offers release from the tyranny of time and opposites. The birth-pangs of the poet's imagination as it creates and is transformed by this illumination are felt in the ten sonnets which closed the volume *25 Poems*. These poems are in his most gnomic and tortuous manner, but it is clear that all the crucial images are of dislocation and transformation of experience, culminating in the apocalyptic restoration of Eden:

> Green as beginning, let the garden diving
> Soar, with its two bark towers, to that Day
> When the worm builds with the gold straws of venom
> My nest of mercies in the rude, red tree.

In the 'Vision and Prayer' sequence, a cycle of twelve pattern poems, this theme is repeated, but where the sonnets are an anthropological ragbag, a veritable witches' sabbath of imagery, these poems compress the mystery of the incarnate redeemer into the traditional and hieratic symbols of the womb, the light, and the blood which is the agony of one and the fire of the other.

Nor are the images of transformation and resurrection confined to obviously religious poems. The 'Ballad of the Long-legged Bait' is, like 'The Rime of the Ancient Mariner', to which it owes a good deal, an allegory of a sort. I wonder what Coleridge would think of it. Its effect at first reading is like a powerful drink mixed of all the other drinks you know, but with a new taste and authority. It would be tedious to demonstrate how the poem recapitulates in a new order Thomas' accustomed imagery, nor am I interested in discovering whether it is indebted to Donne's 'The Bait' (which I suspect) or to Welsh folklore motifs (which I don't know about). The poem records the voyage of a lonely fisherman who uses a girl for bait. She is apparently that object or condition of

44

desire which belongs to the underworld of passion, change and death ruled over by mutability, the irrational female half of the psyche, a sort of Echidna,

> Oh all the wanting flesh his enemy
> Thrown to the sea in the shell of a girl.

She is 'sin who had a woman's shape', fallen Eve, Aphrodite who once risen in a shell is now consigned to the deep. She couples with the creatures under sea, and dies. 'With no more desire than a ghost' the fisherman winds his reel, and 'his decks are drenched with miracles', for the catch is a new world, Eden again, 'a garden holding to her hand', a new creation. Then, as in the Apocalypse, there is 'no more sea'.

> Land, land, land, nothing remains
> Of the pacing, famous sea but its speech,
> And into its talkative seven tombs
> The anchor dives through the floors of a church.

Lost, alone, the fisherman stands 'with his long-legged heart in his hand'.

Among other things, this poem might be a description of the poet's own career. He too fished with the flesh, the live desiring body, in the hidden bottoms of personality; he too caught a haul of miracles, a new world.

The new world was indeed various and beautiful. If the 'holy sonnets' and the 'Ballad' sound as if they had been written by a converted Caliban, the long poem 'A Winter's Tale' was written by Ariel, not half-fish but half-angel. This poem, in some ways the most complete thing he ever did, invites us to a miracle, which the poet attends himself with a kind of ecstasy. It is a fairy tale, and almost tells a story, the story of the union of a lover with his beloved, who is bird or angel. It is the old folk theme of the marriage with the fairy bride. As in Shakespeare's play, the dead comes to life. Locked in loneliness and need, in the grip of wintry sleep, nature and man awake, are transformed by love:

> The dead oak walks for love.
> The carved limbs in the rock
> Leap, as to trumpets. Calligraphy of the old
> Leaves is dancing. Lines of age on the stone weave in a flock. . . .
> For love, the long ago she bird rises. Look.

Nature, history and legend all called, as in apocalypse. The Altamira drawings, the papyri, the marks of man everywhere. And this at the turning of an age, at a birth of the phoenix. Then if we remember that in his tower were heard the voices of leaves, that he graved notes on the time-shaken stone, we can guess that this resurrection is not only of man and history and the self in love but of the poet's art. And the bird is the 'engulfing bride', the goal of desire; but she descends into the winter, into the door of death like the Pentecostal dove. The consummation is 'in the whirlpool at the wanting centre', but also 'in the folds/ Of paradise, in the spun bud of the world'. The snow melts in the fire of the rose; the marriage is a transformation of earthly desire (and perhaps of poetic speech) into heavenly love. What began on a Welsh winter farm ends at the end of Dante's Paradise.

In the world of Dylan Thomas there is no neuter gender, no machinery; nothing is anonymous. It is the world of fairy myth, of nursery rhyme. His heavens are marked by the living creatures of the zodiac, his earth is crossed by seasons as vividly imagined as Spenser's—and it is all himself:

> My grave is watered by the crossing Jordan.
> The Arctic scut, and basin of the South,
> Drip on my dead house garden.
> Who seek me landward, marking in my mouth
> The straws of Asia, lose me as I turn
> Through the Atlantic corn.

And none of this, though it belongs to a pre-scientific cosmology, seems to have been created as a conscious protest against a mechanistic age, but simply 'for the love of Man and in praise of God', as he put it, and also because he couldn't keep still. In a time when many poets write out of symbols recollected in fatigue, stroking their typewriters with a sophisticated and perfunctory caress, the spectacle of this noisy and garrulous primitive is very satisfying. I suppose he will always be caviare to the general, but I think he will escape being breakfast food for the intellectuals, which is a poor fate. For no explication, no eulogy even, can convey the ringing authority of his great moments, when the words which screamed about his sea-tower like gulls, and mocked and maddened him, obey and speak.

Millar MacLure

About 1830 Lamartine pointed to the newspaper as the end of book culture: 'The book arrives too late.'

At the same time Dickens used the press as base for a new impressionist art which D. W. Griffiths and Sergei Eisenstein studied in 1920 as the foundation of movie art.

Robert Browning took the newspaper as art model for his impressionist epic *The Ring and the Book*; Mallarmé did the same in *Un Coup de Dés*.

Edgar Poe, a press man and, like Shelley, a science fictioneer, correctly analysed the poetic process. Conditions of newspaper serial publication led both him and Dickens to the process of writing backwards. This means simultaneity of all parts of a composition. Simultaneity compels sharp focus on *effect* of thing made. Simultaneity is the form of the press in dealing with Earth City. Simultaneity is formula for the writing of both detective story and symbolist poem. These are derivatives (one 'low' and one 'high') of the new technological culture. Simultaneity is related to telegraph, as the telegraph to math and physics.

Joyce's *Ulysses* completed the cycle of this technological art form.

The mass media are extensions of the mechanisms of human perception; they are imitators of the modes of human apprehension and judgement.

Technological culture in the newspaper form structures ordinary unawareness in patterns which correspond to the most sophisticated manoeuvers of mathematical physics.

Newton's *Optics* created the techniques of picturesque and Romantic poetry.

The techniques of discontinuous juxtaposition in landscape poetry and painting were transferred to the popular press and the popular novel.

In 1830, due to this technological revolution, English popular consciousness was structured in ways which French and European intellectuals did not acquire until a later generation.

Average English and American unawareness has been ahead of official culture and awareness for two hundred years; therefore the English and American intellectual for two hundred years has automatically thrown in his lot with the average man against officialdom.

The Swiss cultural historian Sigfried Giedion has had to invent the concept of 'anonymous history' in order to write an account of the new technological culture in Anglo-Saxondom.

The professoriat has turned its back on culture for two hundred years because the high culture of technological society is popular culture and knows no boundaries between high and low.

The children of technological man respond with untaught delight to the poetry of trains, ships, planes, and to the beauty of machine products. In the school room officialdom suppresses all their natural experience; children are divorced from their culture. They are not permitted to approach the traditional heritage of mankind through the door of technological awareness; this only possible door for them is slammed in their faces.

The only other door is that of the high-brow. Few find it, and fewer find their way back to popular culture.

T. S. Eliot has said he would prefer an illiterate audience, for the ways of official literacy do not equip the young to know themselves, the past, or the present.

The technique of an Eliot poem is a direct application of the method of the popular radio-tube grid circuit to the shaping and control of the charge of meaning. An Eliot poem is one instance of a direct means of experiencing, under conditions of artistic control, the ordinary awareness and culture of contemporary man.

Photography and cinema have abolished realism as too easy; they substitute themselves for realism.

All the new media, including the press, are art forms which have the power of imposing, like poetry, their own assumptions. The new media are not ways of relating us to the old 'real' world; they are the real world and they reshape what remains of the old world at will.

Official culture still strives to force the new media to do the work of the old media. But the horseless carriage did not do the work of the horse; it abolished the horse and did what the horse could never do. Horses are fine. So are books.

Technological art takes the whole earth and its population as its material, not as its form.

It is too late to be frightened or disgusted, to greet the unseen with a sneer. Ordinary life-work demands that we harness and subordinate the media to human ends.

The media are not toys; they should not be in the hands of Mother Goose and Peter Pan executives. They can be entrusted only to new artists, because they are art forms.

Harnessing the Tennessee, Missouri, or Mississippi is kid stuff compared to curbing the movie, press, or television to human ends. The wild broncos of technological culture have yet to find their busters or masters. They have found only their P. T. Barnums.

Europeans cannot master these new powers of technology because they take themselves too seriously and too sentimentally. Europeans cannot imagine the Earth City. They have occupied old city spaces too long to be able to sense the new spaces created by the new media.

The English have lived longer with technological culture than anybody else, but they lost their chance to shape it when the ship yielded to the plane. But the English language is already the base of all technology.

The Russians are impotent to shape technological culture because of their inwardness and grimness. The future masters of technology will have to be light-hearted and intelligent. The machine easily masters the grim and the dumb.

At the present moment America is shaping every phase of Russian life and policy by virtue of technological ascendancy.

Russian austerity is based on fear of the new media and their power to transform social existence. Russia stands pat on the status quo ante 1850 that produced Marx. There culture ends. The Russian revolution reached the stage of book culture.

Russian politicians have the same mentality as our professoriat: they wish technology would go away.

We can win China and India for the West only by giving them the new media. Russia will not give these to them.

Television prevents communism because it is post-Marx just as the book is pre-Marx.

Weaver, President of the N.B.C., 'brains' that 'through exposures on television to the great men of his time, the average man will become truly contemporaneous with his age'. This is to slant an important fact. For it has always been an advantage to have direct contact with eminent men, if only because proof positive of their essential mediocrity spurs younger talent. So long as talent is remote from those of eminence, it droops in awe and paralysis. That is the story of 'provincial' cultures. And Weaver is right to note that television helps to make the entire world one city in space. He is just as excited about this as the Italian princelings were about the printing press which, they saw, made them contemporary with the whole human past. It gave them, they felt, a superhuman citizenship in the city of the mighty dead. Renaissance meglomania was thus as much a feature of the new press as ours is tied to the exhibitionism of the camera eye and the new media. And whereas the men of the Renaissance dealt with the past as if it could be re-created as in a Hollywood set, we deal with the cosmos in the same fantasy spirit: we will start real estate schemes for the planets or make a few planets for use and amusement. But the poet remains the only person able to cope with the infinite, interior spaces of our psyche.

To go no further back than Dante, it is instructive to note his management of space. Since his entire work is visual and spatial we can dip at random. The opening of Canto v of the *Inferno* goes:

Thus I descended from the first circle down into the second, which encompasses less space, and so much greater pain, that it stings to wailing.

Here is the generally present visual image of the cone of the Inferno which makes each descending level narrower. But he is just as interested in the auditory and tactual qualities of this space that 'stings to wailing' as in the visual:

We paced along the lonely plain, as one who returning to his lost road, and, till he reached it, seems to go in vain. When we came there where the dew is striving with the sun, being at a place where, in the cool air, slowly it is scattered.

There is no attempt to structure the visual scene beyond the point where phrases like 'the lonely plain' or 'the dew in the sun' become means of instantly evoking mental states. Perhaps Dante employs the visual items of simple melodic phrases, using them to define states of mind as naturally as the notes in a melody do. I think we might even say that his pre-perspective space manner gives some slight priority to the acoustic power of the verbal image. He allows the space images of his words to follow the spherical contours of the acoustic image: he invests or enspheres moments of vision with images. What appears to the eye as a flat space decorated with images and symbols is immediately felt in depth as a boundless inner or mental space.

The famous mirror scene from Canto ii of the *Paradiso* may well be a foretaste of the later perspective art:

Three mirrors thou shalt take, and set two equally remote from thee; and let the third farther removed strike on thine eyes between the other two. Turning to them, have a light set behind thy back, enkindling the three mirrors, and, back-smitten by them all, coming again to thee. Whereas in size the more distant show shall not have so great stretch, yet thou there shalt see it needs must shine as brightly as the others.

Even here it is plain that Dante is not interested in what soon was to become enclosed visual space. Shakespeare's *Sonnet 73* begins:

That time of year thou mayst in me behold
When yellow leaves, or none, or few, do hang
Upon those boughs which shake against the cold,
Bare ruin'd choirs, where late the sweet birds sang.

Here the time of year, designated as a mental state, is visualized swiftly in three different ways in the second line and then a fourth and fifth time in the third and fourth lines. First, bare boughs as choirs for birds of the air, and then ruined abbey choirs, as former scenes of the choirboys' efforts, provide a superimposed visual image. The rapid transition of brief visual shots creates a kaleidoscopic sense of speed and complexity which is controlled only by the solemn music of the lines. Ben Jonson's 'Drink to me only with thine eyes' slows down this visual process greatly, but the control of the spatial items is also in the music rather than any picture-like bounding of the envisioned situation. The ordering of poetic space, as in a picture, did not occur until the theory of the picturesque in painting and of optics in physics had given pause to the forward linear movement of the line.

Wordsworth was an extremely conscious, arty practitioner of the 18th century picturesque theories and techniques, as can be seen in his *Evening Walk, Descriptive Sketches,* and *Solitary Reaper*:

> Behold her, single in the field,
> Yon solitary Highland Lass!
> Reaping and singing by herself;
> Stop here, or gently pass!

His visual instruction or spatial definition is given three times in three lines: 'single', 'solitary', 'by herself'.

The careful use of external landscape to evoke and explore inner states persisted until Rimbaud and the symbolists made the discovery of inner space. But Edgar Poe, as Baudelaire insisted, was the means of bringing this inner space into sharp European focus.

Now the 19th century press and telegraph effected changes in society and communications which we are only beginning to catch up with conceptually. Perhaps what has happened, in the past century especially, has been the completion of the cycle of mechanization of human learning and communication. But that cycle began in pre-history. We become aware of it only at the advanced stage when writing occurs. Writing is the translation of the audible into the visible. The translation is literally, metaphor. Recorded history is thus set upon a metaphor. Before the invention of that metaphor men had been shaping not visual but acoustical space. Oral speech is the articulation of that vague, terrifying ambience by which the ears of archaic man ensphere his being. It is by the visible spacing of pitches that he structures and controls the personal and interpersonal spaces of his world. Until men learned to translate these magical vocal gestures into visual terms, they went in awe and fear of their ordinary breath, their 'winged words'. With writing the emotionally ordered acoustical space of pitch stress gradually dimmed. But even for Aristotle the obvious fact about speech is that it is a technique of arresting the hearer's mind and fixing his attention. For a culture of readers it seems strange to define speech as a series of acoustical gestures for arresting the mind. We had long ceased to speculate on this mystery until the mechanization of speech, image, and gesture brought the wheel full circle. Today, with all our technology, and because of it, we stand once more in the magical acoustical sphere of pre-literate man. Politics have become musical; music has become politics. Government has become entertainment, and vice versa. Commerce has become incantation and magical gesture. Science and magic have married each other. Technology and the arts meet and mingle.

A recent *Fortune* ad is entitled 'Three of a Kind'. We are shown three canny gents in action. The copy begins: 'No beards, no sandals, no long hair, no frantic gestures—but artists just the same. They aren't frenetic movie directors, either, but are art directors for an advertising agency, creating an ad. They know their art all right. Theirs is the toughest job in art—creating.'

It is easy to match that ad by recalling the bizarre invasion of the artist's quarters by the rich after the First War. Wyndham Lewis' analysis of that event in *The Art of Being Ruled* remains a solitary piece of reporting and diagnosis. Today it is not the idle rich but the busy rich who are hastening to acquire squatters' rights all along the art frontiers. Why? Why should the top brass of industry and bureaucracy invade the penurious domain of the solitary artists? Perhaps because technology has itself begun to approach the mystery of the creative process? Because technology has plunged us collectively into the uncharted primitive terrors of individual artistic intuition? Has technology adopted as its province the entire human psyche and the earth which it inhabits? Are there sufficient signs that technological man is prepared to manipulate, as his matter, both earth and spirit? Have the ancient boundaries between art and nature been erased?

Since the mass production of the book began in the 16th century and with the later arrival of the popular press, magazine, movie, radio and television, it has been a tendency for the media to act less as a bridge between the individual and various segments of the outer world than for them to usury the function of that outer world. The new media have blurred the boundaries of inner and outer. The omnipresence of news and views has merged man's inner and outer life. Uninhibited mechanization is totalitarian at many levels. And this fact is merely another facet

54

of the cycle mechanization, in returning us to the state of collectivized, emotional consciousness of archaic man.

For a century it has been evident in North America that great frustration of mind and purpose has resulted from the gap between official and unofficial education. Official institutional instruction at all levels has tried to maintain the priority of traditional verbal and written culture. Unofficial culture has been mainly non-verbal and visual. Unofficially the young have responded spontaneously and enthusiastically to the new technological environment. Their sensibilities have been shaped by the new machine forms which are themselves the product of the artistic imagination in mathematics and physics. But these forms and the popular culture linked to them have no official recognition in the traditional curriculum of verbal culture. A few Europeans like LeCorbusier and Giedion have undertaken to verbalize our technology for us. A few of our artists such as Poe, Henry James, Pound, and Eliot have in reverse order undertaken to technologize the traditional verbal world of the European.

There does exist, then, a two-way bridge between the traditional and technological worlds which are at war in Western culture. But it has been officially ignored or condemned. To travel this bridge requires of the traveller an acquantance with the language and techniques of poetry on the one hand, and of the language and techniques of painting, architecture, and the visual world on the other. Few are prepared to acquire both languages and so the war between these worlds continues, waged witlessly in classroom and market-place alike—witless because nobody stands to gain and because it would cease automatically if the combatants knew it existed. The arts provide us with observational balloons from which to observe this conflict.

It is not an accident that Poe and Dickens appeared as titans of artistic invention to such artists as Baudelaire and Dostoevsky. Why, on the other hand, does the English world regard them as mere popular entertainers? The answer is simple: both Poe and Dickens projected in their writings the verbal equivalent of the commercialized technology which surrounded them. Dickens was a newspaperman at a time when the new impressionist devices of news coverage had been adopted to feed the high-speed steam-presses of London. English industrial technology was more advanced than European poetry and painting. Moreover English poetry and painting of the 18th century were decades ahead of the European equivalents. That is, Thomson, Blake, Sterne, Wordsworth and Shelley were using techniques of landscape for the precise delineation and control of mental stages long before the Europeans. And it was

Newton's *Optics* which gave these techniques in poetry and painting such early impetus. The discovery of the exact correspondence between the structure of the inner eye and the outer world established the study and vogue of symbolic correspondence between landscape and mental states. That technical priority was enjoyed by English poetry and painting almost until the time of Rimbaud and Cézanne. But with Rimbaud and Cézanne came the re-discovery of that inner space, of which from other points of view Dante was the master.

The revolutionary switch from the outer space of Romantic poetry to the inner spaces of symbolist art meant the discovery of the simultaneity of many times and many spaces in the inner landscapes of the mind. The juxtaposition of such times and spaces provided the form of *Illuminations*, *Ulysses* and *The Waste Land*. But such juxtapositions had long been present in the *form* of the 19th century newspaper. News coverage of the globe, made possible by the instantaneity of the telegraph, abridged external space more fantastically than Picasso ever did. The juxtaposition on a single page of human interest stories from every culture of the globe reshaped the whole urban sensibility. The consciousness of industrial man was daily formed by the jostling of many lives and many cultures. His individual life was no longer framed by the experience and perspectives of a single community or a continuous memory of a single people. The artists leaped, as always, to seize the advantages of this change, and to interpret them to men's thoughts and feelings. Poe and Dickens, however, made their move not at the privileged level of the art consciousness of a capital such as Paris. They already lived in the new conditions of collective consciousness from which the sharp individual articulation of awareness had disappeared or in which it was insignificant. London assumed this character by 1780. America was, as a continent, in this state from the same period.

As technology advances, verbalization declines—verbalization, that is to say, of the esthetic or human meaning and implications of technology. It needed a great poet-painter like Wyndham Lewis to bring the English mind (some of it) to the verbal level of awareness of this century. Book culture, which was all that came to America from Europe, was an excellent matrix for technological development, but proved mainly useless in educating eye and ear to emotional literacy about technology.

It was the English poets of the 18th century who rebelled against the linear perspectives of the printed page and who explicitly attacked book culture as an unconscious block in the sensibility of their time. Coleridge pointed out that the poetry of his own day was tending towards the flat landscape of the Chinese painters. Let us keep in mind that pictographic and ideogrammic cultures appear, unlike alphabetic ones, to be able to retain the acoustic speech pitches of pre-literate man. And acoustic cultures seem to be easily and naturally at home in inner space. Related to this, somehow, is the mysterious fact that poetry, whether Anglo-Saxon or contemporary, which develops the visual image intensely, also tends strongly towards the auditory stress. Dylan Thomas is a relevant instance, and we know how effective his work becomes on radio or gramophone. So is Pound: who, for example, was attracted to translate the Anglo-Saxon poem, *The Seafarer*:

> Bitter breast-cares have I abided,
> Known on my keel many a care's hold,
> And dire sea-surge, and there I oft spent
> Narrow nightwatch nigh the ship's head
> While she tossed close to cliffs.

His *Cantos*, from the same point of view, are a flat landscape compounded of innumerable inner and acoustical spaces. In fact, most of the small pieces of that huge architecture are scraps of conversation which comprise 'the tale of the tribe':

> And they want to know what we talked about?
> '*de litterés et de armis, praestantibusque ingeniis,*
> Both of ancient times and our own; books, arms
> And men of unusual genius . . .

Even more than the *Cantos, Finnegans Wake* is the ultimate whispering gallery of the human psyche, its vast nocturnal caverns reverberating with every sigh and gesture of the human mind and tongue since the beginning of time. Joyce had only to remove the date-line from an ordinary newspaper in order to turn its contents into such a timeless whispering gallery-cum-shooting alley. But it is probably the exceptional auditory powers of Joyce and Pound that led them to acoustical manipulation of the great flat landscapes of Romantic art and the new media. To order visual images in the airy dimensions of the inner ear has been their achievement. Perhaps it is this rediscovery of inner acoustical space that led Baudelaire to make the gesture of taking the 'hypocrite lecteur' into his poem. As industrial society excluded the poet, the poet devoured the society.

Not any art doctrine, then, but such complex changes as occur in the emergence of the press as art form, lead to the union of the visual and acoustical space in a new space-time poetry.

Marshall McLuhan

Memorandum: To Television Producers, X & Y Company Shows

In general, the moral code of the characters in our dramas will be that of the bulk of the Canadian middle class, as it is commonly understood. The usual middle-class taboos on sex subjects will be observed. Material dealing with sex perversion, miscegenation, and rape is banned, as are scenes of excessive passion and suggestive dialogue. Suggestive situations covered by innocuous dialogue should not be used.

Scripts should be checked to insure that lines with conscious or unconscious ambiguities are eliminated.

There should be no profanity or near-profanity. Slang of the more vulgar type will be avoided.

The treatment of unpleasant material shall always be within the bounds of good taste. This applies particularly to accidents; executions as legal punishment for crimes; brutality or gruesomeness of any sort.

Detailed information on the mechanics of any criminal procedure either in dialogue or narration is banned. Crime shall not be presented in such a manner as to inspire sympathy or encourage imitation.

Intoxicants will not be mentioned. Whether or not a particular character is permitted to drink or to show the influence of drink must be a matter of judgment; the type of character, type of show, and general context must be considered in making this judgment.

The X & Y Company prefers that criminal murder, suicide, or kidnapping should not be used to motivate plot or resolve plot conflicts. Should murder or suicide be necessary, it is suggested that they take place off-stage.

Ministers, priests, and similar representatives of positive social forces shall not be cast as villains or represented as committing a crime, or placed in any unsympathetic or anti-social role.

Omissions: If it is necessary in the development of conflict for a character to attack some basic concept of the Canadian way of life, *a complete and convincing defence of the concept attacked must be made in the same broadcast.*

No material will be broadcast which may give offence either directly or by inference to any recognized social, political, religious, educational, or athletic organization.

There will be no criticism or endorsements of political parties.

There will be no material which can be construed as derogatory to any religion or race, or which may foment racial or religious strife.

Material which depends upon physical imperfections or deformities for humorous effect is not acceptable.

There will be no controversial material referring to sharply-drawn national or regional issues, nothing slurring any occupation, no ridicule of sectional manners and fashions.

We will avoid any reference to the past conflicts between the French and English Canadians. Wherever possible, we will foster the establishment of a stronger friendship between both races.

Facetious treatment of subjects normally regarded as serious will be avoided.

When appropriate, dramatic characters will be portrayed as recognizing and accepting world tension. Scenes that tend to lower public morals are not acceptable.

There will be no material on any of our programs which could in any way further the concept of business as cold, ruthless, and lacking all sentiment or spiritual motivation. If a businessman is cast in the role of a villain, it must be made clear that he is not typical, but is as much despised by his fellow business men as he is by other members of society.

TACTILE COMMUNICATION

The skin serves both as receptor and transmitter of messages, some of which are culturally defined. Its acute sensitivity allows the development of such an elaborate system as Braille, but tactilism is more basic than such oddities imply, and constitutes a fundamental communication form.

In infancy there is recognition and response first to *signals*, then to *signs*, finally to *symbols*. The infant arrives with a repertory of biological signals; he responds to these in patterns of reflexes such as Moro, Babinski, coughing, yawning, sneezing, swallowing, and so on. When two signals are received more or less concomitantly, as in a conditioned reflex experiment, the second, so-called unconditioned and previously indifferent signal, may become the surrogate or sign for the first. Still later the infant learns that these signs are not only defined by others, but that their appropriate responses are defined as well. And thus he begins to use culturally patterned tactile symbols.

In time this early form of communication is augmented by speech; in part it may lay the foundation for learning speech. The mother will console her infant by patting him, later by both pats and words, and finally, from the other room, 'It's all right, Johnny. I'm right here.'

Tactile communication is never wholly superseded; it is merely elaborated by the symbolic process. Cassirer remarks, 'Vocal language has a very great technical advantage over tactile language; but the technical defects of the latter do not destroy its essential use.' In some interpersonal relations it communicates more fully than speech, *e.g.*, consoling a bereaved person, when 'words fail'. In *After Many a Summer Dies the Swan*, Huxley writes, 'The direct animal intuitions aren't rendered by words; the words merely remind you of your memories of similar experience.' I may say I have an intuitive *feeling*, that it was a *touching* experience, and thus refer to an earlier and perhaps more basic medium than language itself.

The Skin

Tactual sensitivity is probably the most primitive sensory process, appearing as tropism or thigmotaxis in the lowest organism. Many infrahuman organisms orient themselves by feelers or antennae by which they *feel* their way through life. It is also of major importance in human life.

The human skin, with only vestigial body hair, is probably more sensitive than that of other mammals, although movement of the hair can stimulate cutaneous sensations by follicular displacements: stroking 'against the grain' may tickle, 'with the grain', prove soothing. Petting the baby rhythmically not only soothes him, but apparently promotes his well-being and metabolic efficiency. Caressing, also rhythmic, is of immense significance in adult life.

Rats which have been gentled are better able to metabolize food and are less susceptible to various forms of shock, experimentally produced convulsions, and so on. Those raised from birth with a cardboard ruff around their necks to prevent them from licking their own bodies are unable to care for their young by licking them. Kittens cannot urinate or defecate unless the mother licks the anus or urethra and thereby elicits evacuation.

Orbelli found what he called 'sympathetic connections' from the skin to the smooth muscle of the intestines which provide pathways for the conduction of soothing, licking stimulation to these highly motile organs. The gut, from mouth to anus, is lined with epithelial cells not unrelated to the skin and derived from the same embryological layer. Moreover, the end organs for tactile stimuli are richly provided in and around the mouth and anus, and in the genitals, and are numerous or sensitive in the skin adjacent to these parts. Orbelli's findings have not been confirmed, yet it is difficult to see how tactile soothing operates unless there are other modes of conduction than the presently recognized sensory processes of warm-cold, pain, and pressure.

We can say that the skin, as a communication organ, is highly complex and versatile, with an immense range of functional operations and a wide repertory of responses. These can only be understood by assuming a more richly endowed sensory-nervous system than the warm-cold-pain-pressure categories: probably the sympathetic innervation of the sweat glands and capillaries is conductive to the viscera and perhaps to other organ systems. Insofar as capillary dilation and constriction by cold or warmth either initiate or accelerate alterations in the circulation of the blood, tactile stimulation—especially rhythmic caressing—may prove a major component of the homeostatic process. A person in fear or pain may recover his physiological equilibrium through tactual contacts with a sympathetic person.

Bott once showed that the third finger was passively the most sensitive to a hair aesthesiometer, while the forefinger was much more sensitive when used purposefully to detect a hair concealed under a cigarette paper. In other words, an individual has a selective, variable tactile awareness, not unrelated to purposive conduct.

Personality Development

Tactual sensitivity appears early in foetal life as probably the first sensory process to become functional. The foetus more or less floats in the amniotic fluid, and continuously receives the rhythmic impacts of the maternal heart beat, impinging on the skin of his whole body and magnified by the fluid. His own heart beat will later synchronize or be out of tune with the maternal heart beat; in either case he experiences a series of impacts upon his skin to which he develops a continuous response, as a physiological resonance. Thus, even before birth he adjusts to a rhythmically pulsating environment. At birth he experiences pressures and constrictions, which are sometimes intense, and then suddenly he is exposed to atmospheric pressures and an altered temperature, which evoke respiratory activity and presumably a number of tactile responses.

The newborn mammal 'needs' to be nuzzled, cuddled and licked by its mother; it remains close to her body, receiving warmth and close tactual contacts, plus frequent licking and nursing. The treatment of the human infant may conform to this pattern or depart drastically from it. Some infants are kept close to the mother, may be given the colostrum, allowed to nurse freely and as long as desired; others may have such tactile contacts sharply curtailed. But in most instances the child is nuzzled and licked and patted rhythmically; he touches his lips to his mother's body, more specifically to the nipple, and increasingly fingers her body. By such means he evokes from her the stimulation which he 'needs': warmth, milk, and so on.

It seems probable that the newborn infant, with its undeveloped, inadequate capacity for homeostasis, requires these experiences for maintenence of his internal equilibrium. Thus, he keeps warm through bodily contacts; he maintains, or recovers, his equilibrium when disturbed by fear, pain, hunger, or cold through rhythmic tactual stimulation like patting, stroking, caressing. The emotionally disturbed infant usually responds with increasing composure to patting or even vigorous, but rhythmic, slapping on the back. What might awaken or keep awake an older child, puts an infant to sleep; this age difference supports the assumption of an early infantile sensitivity or need for rhythmic tactual stimulation which fades out or is incorporated into other patterns.

The baby begins to communicate with himself by feeling his own body, exploring its shape and textures, and thereby to establish his body image. Later he focuses his vision upon his feet and fingers and so begins to build up visual images to reinforce tactile experiences.

The quality or intent of the message, as contrasted with its content, may be conveyed by the emotional colouring-tone of voice, facial expression, gesture, or lightness of touch, and the recipient responds largely to this intent or quality. Usually the mother speaks or hums or sings to the child as she pats or cuddles him, and thus he learns to recognize the sound of her voice as a surrogate for her touch. In time her reassuring words are accepted as equivalents of tactile experience, even though she isn't within touching distance. Equally, he may learn to recognize a note of displeasure in her voice and may cringe, as if to physical punishment which he has experienced previously when scolded. It seems clear that his reception of verbal messages is predicated in large measure upon his prior tactile experience.

The baby's initial spatial orientation occurs through tactile explorations: feeling with hands and often with the lips, and testing out the quality, size, shape, texture and density of whatever he can reach. These manipulations involve motor activities and increasingly skilful neuromuscular coordinations, established through tactile messages and gradually replaced by visual cues. Bumps, pain, warmth are primary tactile signals; visual signs—size, shape, appearance, colour—later become their surrogates. It is often forgotten how much prolonged learning was required to master these motor patterns. The adult rarely recalls how, in early life, he relied upon touch for his initial orientation to the spatial dimensions of the world.

Thus the baby's perception of the world is built upon and shaped by tactile experiences. These become increasingly overlaid by other symbolic patterns, so much so that they often become inaccessible, except through such experiences as in the World Game, finger painting, clay modelling, water play, and so on. Perhaps the potency of music and poetry, with their rhythmical patterning and varying intensities of sounds, depends in large measure upon the provision of an auditory surrogate for primary tactile experiences.

The child begins by exploring everything within reach, but gradually he learns that there are prohibitions involving both people and things, and he begins to curtail his contacts. He is taught to impute inviolability to what was previously accessible, and thereby is inducted into the social world with its elaborate codes of respect for property and persons.

Moreover, the child learns to distinguish, first by tactile means, between the 'me' and the 'not-me'. Later he modifies these definitions, casting them largely in verbal form, but the tactile definitions nevertheless remain prior and basic.

Babies seem to differ widely in their need for tactile experiences and in their response to such ministrations. Deprivation of such experiences may compromise the infant's future learning, particularly of speech, and indeed, of all symbolic systems, including more mature tactile communication. If severely limited in these experiences, presumably he must wait until his capacities for visual and auditory communication are developed sufficiently to permit him to enter into satisfactory communication with others.

Such a child may become unusually dependent upon the authority of his parents and overly obedient to their pronouncements; he will lack the experience of prior communication, and he may find the sudden jump not only difficult, but leading to unhealthy relationships. Perhaps this offers clues to schizophrenic personalities who are unable to enter fully and effectively into the symbolic world of others, and who are reported to be rejected babies frequently, deprived of mothering. It may also throw light upon the impairment of abstract thinking observed in children separated from their mothers. There is evidence as well that not only reading disabilities, but speech retardation and difficulties arise from early deprivation of, and confusion in, tactile communication. Such deprivation may evoke exploratory searches for surrogates: masturbation, thumb sucking, fingering the nose, ears, hair, or reliance on other modes of communication.

The child is often alienated from his mother around five or six when this seeking and giving tactual contacts begins to diminish in our culture. We see boys evading or being denied such contacts, although with girls it may continue longer. This diminution of tactual sensitivity and experiences of middle childhood, the so-called latency period, ceases abruptly at puberty when the boy and girl become avid for such contacts, seeking to touch and be touched. In adolescence, tactile communication increases, at first between members of the same sex, as boys walk together with arms on each others' shoulders, girls with arms around each others' waists, and then the first tentative heterosexual explorations. Tactile communication in adult mating has been elaborated by some cultures into extremely complex patterns.

Cultural Patterning

Each culture activates or limits tactile communication not only between its members, but between the individual and his outer world, for at every moment man is communicating with his environment, receiving and responding to stimuli, often without conscious awareness (*e.g.*, pressure on feet or buttocks, cool breezes, smoking).

Skin colour can serve as a visual identification, eliciting responses which are often tactile, *e.g.*, avoiding contacts, the desire to touch, and so on. The amount of clothing, and the parts of the body covered, differ by culture and according to time, place, and occasion. The body arts, including painting, tattooing, incising, and the use of cosmetics generally, are ways of enhancing the skin's appearance, just as grooming the skin, especially mutual grooming, bathing, anointing, perfuming, and shaving are patterns for modifying the skin to indicate tactual readiness for communication. Thus body arts and grooming serve as surrogates for invitations to tactile contacts, real or symbolic; the 'admiring glance' indicates that the message was received, understood, and accepted.

Such decorations are of significance in the performance of roles and allow others to respond appropriately. In large part the masculine and feminine roles are defined by patterns of skin exposure, body arts, clothing, and the kinds of tactile contacts permitted between them. Every culture has a well-established code for such communications. Shame, blushing, and pallor may be associated with their violation; modesty with their observance.

Tactile communication is of importance in the establishment of the inviolability of things and persons under penalties for unsanctioned approach. Indeed, the incest taboo itself, so basic to social organization, is learned primarily in terms of tactile restrictions. The 'don't touch' extends as well to material objects and involves a wide array of property rights;

65

the infant's first eager explorations are channelized and soon he learns not only *who,* but *whose.* Gradually he transforms these parental prohibitions into self-administered inhibitions by learning to perceive things and persons as signs or symbols for avoidance.

It may be safe to say that much of a kinship system, as well as rank, caste, role, age, are learned and maintained in terms of touch. The handshake, with removal of glove, close dancing, rubbing noses, kissing, the arm around the shoulder or waist, all these are sharply defined, as are the tactile experiences of love-making. The texture of food, the 'feel' of a fabric, the temperature of a drink, are defined both culturally and personally. Manufacturers report difficulty in marketing products which meet all requirements, save that of 'feeling right': metal furniture feels too cold, plastic dinnerware too light. We even judge a painting, not only on form, colours, and content, but by texture, by how it would feel if we touched it. Perhaps our appreciation of sculpture is reduced by the art gallery sign: 'Do Not Touch'.

Communication with the self by masturbation is probably universal, but sanctioned by only some cultures. Other forms of tactile communication with the self are tics, scratching, patting the hair, pressing against objects, and massage, the last also being the focus of professional practices. Finally, each culture sets patterns of painful experiences that must be accepted: spanking, slapping the face, fire walking or handling, scarification, stoical acceptance of cold or wounds.

Highly abstract concepts seem to lie outside the range of most tactile messages and probably occur only in such a system as Braille.

Lawrence K. Frank

The *Poema del Cid*—I may remind readers whose encyclopedias are out of reach—is a Spanish epic of 3730 lines written in the year 1140 or thereabouts.[1] With an historical veracity unparalleled in the heroic poetry of the Middle Ages, it tells of the exile from Castille of Rodrigo Díaz de Vivar first called the Cid (Sidi) by his Moorish antagonists. As a result of calumny and court jealousy, the King of Castille and León, Alfonso VI, 'takes away his love' from the hero and so condemns him to a kind of social banishment. Even worse, he orders him and his small band of relatives and followers to leave the kingdom within a given time limit. They go to the one place where such ancestors of the 'conquistadores' could go, over the border to live by their courage and wits among the Moors. The first of the three 'cantares' gives a moving account of the Cid's initial poverty, of his first skirmishes and scuffles, and of

---

[1] The present article is derived from a monograph of some 150 pages to be published in Spanish. Yet it is not an abstract. It is rather a special simplified version, a kind of report of research activity, prepared in the hope of interesting readers not primarily concerned with Old Spanish literature. Hence, it has much more conclusion than fact — and what facts there are have been severely foreshortened. May I request those who for good or ill may wish to quote me to keep these reservations in mind. And may I apologize in advance to professional students of the *Poema*. The editor's repeated urging to submit this preliminary report and the possibility he offered of finding readers outside of our own field were irresistibly tempting.

his almost picaresque self-defence against two hostile societies. The last two 'cantares' record his increasing prosperity, his return to favour, and his capture of Valencia as a fief—an event that was the marvel of the age.

The end of the *Poema* is deeply in accord with Max Scheler's doctrine that the hero by definition 'enriches' the world in value. The anonimous 'juglar' in a series of moving episodes shows how the meaning of Spain— not just Castille but, for the first time, all Spain—has been enhanced by the Cid's version of heroism. He is not irrational and passionately savage as are the inhabitants of the *Nibelungenlied* nor yet an individualist of incredible prowess and incredible rashness such as Roland. Rather he is practical, a family man, a natural leader with a humorous human touch unique in the Mediaeval world. He is a man of sure moderate judgement and natural dignity, qualities which remind us more of the frontiersman (as given in our national typology) than of the knight. When all of this has been fully displayed in action and dialogue, one of the last verses makes explicit the meaning his person—not just his conquests and deeds —has for his people: 'a todos alcança ondra por el que en buena nació'.[1]

It is the Cid of the *Poema* who sets for Spain the human pattern of national values, who first represents the positing of honour on the 'integral' self-maintenance of the individual in all adverse circumstances. In this the jovial and heroically successful Cid is one with the sad ever-defeated knight of the Mancha. The Cid has fulfilled his epic function for his people.

The form of the *Poema* is exceedingly irregular. Written for chanted recital on three successive evenings, its verses are of uneven length and rhyme assonantally in equally uneven stanzas. 'Laisses' is the technical term. The grammar, too, is fluid in its tracing of heroic movement. Connectives are missing; short clauses and sentences succeed each other without regard for transition; and the morphological forms vary from verse to verse. But most irregular of all—so irregular as to be almost chaotic—are the tenses of the verbs. The two regular Spanish past tenses, the preterite and the imperfect, frequently disregard the dis-tinction of time of action driven with so much difficulty into the minds and habits of foreign students. That is to say, the 'juglar' seldom makes it clear that one shows past condition and the other past conclusion. He is quite capable of replacing 'Once upon a time there was [imperfect] a king who built [preterite] a tower . . .' with its reverse. Even more confusing is the frequent intermixture of presents and present perfects

---

[1] 'Honour comes to all because of him who was born in a good hour.' This is one of the favorite epic epithets for the Cid and serves, as we shall see, as a kind of enhanced proper name.

68

into the narrative stream. The following passage (translated literally and so incorrectly) will serve as an example:

They *loosed* [preterite] the reins; they *think* to go.
Near *approaches* the deadline for leaving the kingdom.
My Cid *came* [preterite] to rest in Spinaz de Can.
Many warriors *come* into his service that night from around about.
The next day he *thinks* to ride.
The loyal Cid *is going* out of his country,
on the left Sant Estevan, a goodly city;
he *passed* [preterite] through Alcobiella which *is* already
the end of Castille;
the highroad of Quinea, he *was going* [imperfect] to cross.

Traditionally this crazy quilt of tenses has been understood as a sign of the 'popularity' of the Cid's epic—a sign of its use of a 'popular' language to tell its story. Although the 'Volksgeist' was long ago consigned to the history of ideas, the basic classification of poetry—particularly epic poetry—into 'popular' and 'cultivated' brackets is still with us. And one of the accepted signs of such 'popularity' is the indiscriminate and uncalculated use of the 'historical present' to make the narrative more 'vivid'.[1] The 'popular' mind—and this may be taken to mean the mind of a poet writing for and in terms of a 'popular' audience—is as unmindful of the rules for sequence of tenses as a Grandma Moses is of the rules of perspective. There is no narrative point of view (to use a notion often applied to the art of that most 'cultivated' of narrators, Henry James) from which tenses can relate themselves logically to each other. As a result, the 'popular' poet uses tense according to the impulse of the moment—or, at best, according to his instinctive appreciation of the dramatic needs of the moment. An untutored genius, he writes a language of vital expression, a poetry that is free from grammatical awareness of time and space. In the words of Jacob Grimm, such a poet offers us the fabulous gift of 'life itself in pure action'.

There can be no question but that this is an attractive theory. It has all the charm of the Romanticism it reflects, all the appeal of a myth of lost freedom. Even more, as I shall try to show, it is not entirely mistaken! It is incomplete; it has been wrongly emphasized in certain respects; yet it corresponds to a certain underlying truth. Let us see first the mistaken emphasis. Bergson insists that the sequence from preliminary

---

[1] There is a kind of unquestioned rapprochement of the 'historical present' as used in popular speech to the mixture of tenses not only of the *Poema del Cid* but also to that of the *Chanson de Roland*, its fellow 'chansons de gestes', as well as an infinite number of Spanish 'romances' or ballads. The fact of irrational mixture distinguishes this kind of 'historical present' from the more systematic, and so more 'cultivated', use of the present by a Virgil. Actually, as I shall try to show, Virgil seems to me much closer to a 'popular' use of the present than these Mediaeval poems.

chaos to natural order, an habitual mental sequence derived from the myth of creation, is the cause of a great deal of erroneous thinking. There is always order, even though it may be unrecognizable from the point of view of the observer. A child's room cluttered with toys will serve as an example. The strewing of blocks and lead soldiers reflects not random disarray but the vital course of the child's existence in the room. This, I think, is the error of the neo-Romantic interpretation of the 'popular' historical present. Like wistful adults, such critics view the *Poema* and poems resembling it from the point of view of an age trapped in time, space, and grammar and conscious of the trap. Hence, they stress the lost freedom to be disorderly—even cutely anarchical —and ignore the possibility of another kind of order quite alien to conventional narrative practice. 'Freedom from' has been emphasized more than 'freedom to . . .'

A chance observation first indicated to me that such a hidden system or order might be found in the *Poema del Cid*.[1] I happened to notice that the sequence of tenses was regular and unexceptional (from the point of view of standard grammar) *in the dialogue*. And that means in about 45 percent of the lines according to the tabulation of a German scholar. Here, I thought, was a striking demonstration that the mixture of present and past was not a matter of linguistic naiveté. Instead the poet seemed to have two distinct ways of using tense: when the hero speaks he does so from his heroic point of view and the tenses take their normal course. But when he himself narrates, he seems to discard his point of view (in this the Romantic interpretation is correct) in favour of some other principle of tense arrangement. The poet, as we shall see, reverently refrains from 'possessing' the hero and his deeds from the temporal perspective of the present. He refrains from chaining them to an irrevocable past by adherence to the grammatical logic of his narrative position.[2]

At this point the question could be posed directly: what was the order of tenses in the narrative? If not vital hazard, what did each tense actually signify? The answer involved a survey of the narrative language into the details of which I need not here enter. My effort was to try

---

[1] For the *Chanson de Roland* (and presumably for other 'chansons de geste') Anna Granville Hatcher has published sensitive and brilliant stylistic analyses of tense usage. Her interpretation, however, is based on a narrative quite different from the Spanish and so cannot be adapted for my purposes. See 'Tense Usage in the *Roland*', *Studies in Philology*, 1942, and 'Epic Patterns in Old French', *Word*, 1946.

[2] Theorists agree (and the notion goes back as far as Hesiod according to Bowra) that the epic refers by its very nature to a past Epic Age, to a past of super-human 'Homeric' virtue and prowess. Yet the very stressing of this pastness involves a counter-stress on 'presentation', on 'invoking' for present wonder and possible imitation. The past is important to the present and becomes a myth to be relived by the present. It must not, therefore, be thought of archaeologically or picturesquely (in the manner of a Scott). That is to say it must not be thought of as wholly and irretrievably past.

70

to discover the linguistic circumstances most frequently accompanying the several tenses in their ordinary usage. After months of painful tabulation, I arrived at one suggestive relationship: when the hero was the named subject of the sentence (a very frequent situation in this as in all epics), the preterite tense was used four times as much as the present.[1] Conversely, when the subject has no proper name (this included things, groups of people, and, very very infrequently, personal pronouns in the singular) the present replaced the preterite by a margin almost as wide. Thus, these two tenses seemed to depend more on the subject of the sentence than on the time—past or present—of action. There was here an apparent principle of stylistic order—apart from the poet's 'popular' or 'naive' freedom to circumvent time.

Readers familiar with non-civilized cultures (or with the cover to the second issue of this journal) will have already suspected the nature of this principle. They will have recognized in this subject-tense correlation a sign of the extraordinary—and frequently magical—importance which the name can have. This is specially true of heroic poetry from the *Iliad* to the ballads of our own time. In poetry as well as magic, the name is in a real sense an invocation which brings the hero and his deeds up out of the past. It is not a sign. It belongs to the heroic essence —and it is significant in this connection that the warcry of the Cid is a kind of self-invocation. The Spanish hero brings terror to the Moors and courage to his own handful of fellow exiles by proclaiming: 'I am Ruy Díaz, the Cid of Bivar, the Fighter.' It is a name which the poet never tires of using (with numberless variations of epithet) and which the listener never tires of hearing. It is his assurance that the epic is not a fiction but rather encloses profound and specific human truth. Only in his name can a hero be 'celebrated' epically, for only in his name can his unique individual value be expressed. Praise and flattery imply comparison, elevation of the person praised on a given hierarchy of values, whereas heroism is essentially incomparable. The hero creates values in his action, values so unique that their praise is impossible. They can only be 'celebrated' in the naming of the doer and his deeds. In this sense, one might call 'A rose is a rose is a rose' a 'celebrative' lyric.[2]

But why the preterite tense? Castro remarks in the *Structure of Spanish History*[3] that the grammar of the *Poema* is axiological rather than

---

[1] The same thing holds true for the secondary heroes as well as other properly named subjects.

[2] One of the most striking results of this heroic uniqueness is the fact that heroes are so frequently bad from the point of ethics (that is to say, systematized values). Although the Cid is far removed from a Hagen or a Raoul de Cambrai in this sense, he can stoop to a picaresque confidence trick without the slightest self-questioning.

[3] This book, replete with seed intuitions for the human sciences, has just been published in translation by the Princeton Press. Its profound integration of history with culture, deserves the attention of anthropologists and sociologists as well as historians.

logical. As a narrative, its parts are arranged in terms of value estimations (like a mediaeval painting in which the most important saint is the biggest) and not in terms of sequence and consequence. In other words, the preterite is the tense of action by the named hero because it expresses in some way the special value of his action. It is a tense which communicates importance instead of time—a tense which is not really a 'tense' at all, just as the gold of a painted halo is not really a colour. The present, on the other hand, used with those sentence subjects which are not 'celebrated' in their names is of lesser value. Rather than narrating more vividly (as the 'historical present' is supposed to do) it is a filler tense, a background tense from which the preterites stand out in stylistic relief.

These statements are mere assumptions—as vague as the Romantic generalizations they replace—until they are realized in our experience with the text. Since here such an experience must be prefabricated, the following will have to do. The Cid is sleeping in his palace in Valencia; a lion has escaped from the palace zoo:

> The followers of the Cid *furl* their capes on their arms,
> And they *surround* the couch of their lord; they *stay* there
> [to protect him] . . .
> At this moment He who was born in a good hour *awoke,*
> *saw* his couch surrounded by his good vassals:
> 'What is this men? What do you want?'
> 'Oh, honored sir, the lion frightened us.'
> My Cid *leaned* on his elbow; rose to his feet;
> *has* his own cape hanging at his neck; and *headed* straight for the
> lion.

The feeling for tableau, for pictorial hierarchy, is evident even in this fragment of episode; but we must also notice that its movement—in accord with the demands of the genre—is continuous. On the one hand, there is the movement of the nameless vassals described by the narrator in the present tense. On the other, there is the preterite action sequence of the hero who 'awoke', who 'saw', who 'raised himself on one elbow' (to see the lion), who 'rose to his feet', and 'who headed straight for the lion'. There is something special, something self-determined in this decisive preterite action—action of which each gesture and successive phase is underlined for our admiration. If the vassals are described in the present, the Cid is celebrated in the preterite. There is, of course, one apparent exception, the cape which the Cid 'has hanging' at his neck in the present (since he disdains to protect himself with it as do his vassals). Yet this is precisely something which the Cid doesn't do, action which he refuses to accomplish, and, hence, hardly to be celebrated.

Both the narrative movement—with its almost pictorial contrast of vassal to lord—and the narrative grammar—with its contrast of present and preterite tenses—are clearly axiological.

Confronted with this rejection of the 'historical present', the surprised grammarian will hardly admit that 'axiology' is an acceptable substitute. If the temporal interpretation of tense is to be discarded, he will ask, what replaces it? Or more simply, why and how is the preterite used as if it were more valuable than the present? My answer is one that is suggested by contemporary trends of grammatical thinking: the tenses of the *Poema* are used aspectually, as if they were not tenses at all but aspects. The preterite is, of course, traditionally perfective. It expresses concluded, accomplished, 'perfect' action—that is to say, the kind of action that constitutes the heroic 'deed'. The hero doesn't doubt, feel moody, or exist inconclusively. The antithesis of a hypochondriac, psychic delay is alien to his being. His value resides in doing, in completing acts one after another, and there can be no question but that the perfectivity of the preterite becomes him. As for the present, its failure to indicate completion one way or another suits better those nameless subjects whose role is not to start and finish action on their own but to obey. It is the tense of those subjects who are described—like the worried vassals of the lion episode—as they arrange themselves about the heroic prime mover.[1]

This notion of evaluative or stylistic aspects is confirmed neatly by the verbs which are used with the Cid as subject. A French linguist remarks that 'there are certain verbs for which a story teller will abandon past time and go into the present: *ill entre, il sort, il part, il s'arrête . . .*'[2] The historical present is for orthodox grammatical thinking a means to vivid energetic action and only disappears when the 'life' of the story is 'suspended in favour of description'. The point is that the verbs which specialize in the historical present are not at all the same as those put into the present in the *Poema*. The French verbs listed are all perfective, verbs which conclude themselves as they are used, while in the *Poema* the verbs preferring the present (three to one over the preterite) are imperfective: 'to think', 'to go', 'to be able', 'to have'. They are verbs which denote a process or condition instead of an act begun and finished. Conversely, it is the 'active, vivid, energetic, lively' verbs which are used with the Cid and put into the preterite (70 and 80 percent of the

---

[1] As I have already mentioned, this category of 'nameless' subjects includes not only the groups, the vassals and soldiers under the Cid's command, but also singular and even inanimate subjects. All together these things make up the narrative world, a world which, unlike that of the novel, is never described for its own sake. Within the epic narrative its only purpose is to be acted upon and to provide a place for heroism. It is just the opposite of an 'environment' and so refrains from creating experience or influencing action.

[2] Buffin, *La durée et le temps en français*, Paris. Buffin elaborates upon but does not contradict the accepted notion of the historical present as presented, for example, by a Brugmann.

time). The situation is, in fact, just the reverse of that which the notion of historical present might lead us to expect. The most familiar use of the English 'popular' historical present is with the verb 'to say': 'he says . . . and then she says . . .' But in the *Poema* 'decir' is used 92 times in the preterite and only 17 times in the present.[1]

Thus, the Cid not only has his own tense but also his own kind of verbs. He is an active agent not only in the story but also in the way the story is told. With his high frequency of preterites and with his overwhelming choice of perfective verbs, he penetrates the very process of narration. In the invocation of his name—mío Cid Ruy Díaz de Bivar, el que en buen ora çinxo espada—he dominates one sentence after another and almost seems to push the narrator aside. This is, of course, not a new thing to say about epic poetry. In one of the most famous passages of the *Laocöon*, Lessing remarks on the 'active' poetry of the *Iliad*. Homer, he says, does not himself describe how Agamemnon is dressed; rather he lets the hero put on his clothes item by item as the active named subject of the narrative.[2] Heroes are beyond description; they can only be celebrated in their autonomous self-generated action, in their 'activation' of the poetic narrative. As for their poets, they have traditionally relegated themselves to anonimity. In the words of the Spanish novelist, Valle Inclán, they 'write on their knees'.

Such, I maintain, is the hidden order of the tenses in the *Poema del Cid*. When the Cid is subject he is celebrated with perfective verbs and in a perfective tense; he is celebrated insofar as he initiates and completes deeds in his own name. But when the persons and artifacts of the narrative world take command of the sentences, the verbs are imperfective and the tense present. The poet no longer need stand aside in an attitude of celebrative reverence. He can describe 'background' (perhaps 'foundation' or 'circumstance' would be better words) with direct and dramatic effectiveness. The two major tenses of the *Poema* are, thus, two aspects, perfective and imperfective.[3] They are also stylistic indicators of narrative importance and as such they correspond to alternate attitudes of admiration and intervention—celebration and description—on the part of the poet. He enters in the present and withdraws in the preterite, thereby converting the two tenses into 'stylistic aspects'. That is to say,

---

[1] The use of 'decir' in the present is frequent in other non-epic genres of Old Spanish poetry — such as the famous *Libro de buen amor*. But in the *Poema* the value of saying cannot be communicated by the present. 'Then he says . . . ' implies an attitude quite antithetical to 'Achilles spoke winged words . . . '.

[2] There is an identical treatment of the Cid's dress in the *Poema*. It is a coincidence beyond the range of conceivable influence which may be attributed to the generic similarity of the two narratives. Gestures and dress are as well as battles the recurrent foci of epic celebration.

[3] The third major tense, the imperfect, is also used aspectually, a situation which will hardly surprise contemporary theorists who have in several different ways sought to divorce this tense from time. Its function in the *Poema* is quite distinct from the present, however — as I try to show in the monograph on which this article is based.

aspects which, like all classic components of style, reflect the prevailing value level or 'decorum' of the poem.[1]

The *Poema del Cid* is unquestionably an epic and reflects in its style the recurrent conditions of epic creation. It is also unique, as unique in its use of tense as in its moderate historical hero. And I may conclude this discussion with some uneducated guessing as to why and how. The only text I know in Spanish which uses tense in a fashion at all similar to the *Poema* is a 16th century translation of the *Song of Songs*. In his commentary the translator, the exquisite humanist, poet, and mystic, Fray Luis de León, indicates that he uses the preterite to render the Hebrew intensive aspect—in spite of all temporal anomaly. And if this is consciously done in the 16th century, is it not possible that a Castille which had already 'coexisted' with Semitic culture for four centuries should more or less unconsciously assimilate Semitic aspects to its narrative techniques? Castro's brilliant discussion of the interpenetration of Moorish and Christian cultures gives the strongest kind of support to such an assumption.[2] And Edmund Wilson's remarks on the intensives of the Old Testament by this time sound familiar:

When Enoch or Noah 'walks with God', he does so in this form of the verb 'to walk' and nobody has ever known how to render it. Yet one gets from the Hebrew original the impression that the walking of these patriarchs was of a very special kind, that it had the effect of making them more important and more highly charged.[3]

My guess—uneducated because I know no aspectual language at first hand—is precisely this: that aspect, in the Semitic Orient a means of value communication, has been assimilated in typical Spanish fashion to the primary Occidental genre, the epic.[4] The epic was, indeed, the one kind of narrative to which aspects could be assimilated, for as the Romantics knew, it lacked a point of view, a single perspective from

---

[1] In the narrative style of the *Poema*, it is, of course, impossible to 'fix' a given tense, to establish a single connotation which will hold for its every occurrence. Many preterites are used in a manner which would be hard to distinguish from that of an ordinary narrative — the temporal use of tense being a recurrent possibility for the poet. In other individual cases, the preterite seems only to indicate perfectivity and to each special evaluative commitment. Finally, there are a great many instances (such as those translated from the lion episode) in which the indication of conclusion is less important than the indication of value or importance. These are the most interesting stylistically, and may be understood as a kind of 'intensive'. For the determination of these qualities, ordinary linguistic and statistical analysis is insufficient. The curious feature of such a study as this is that it begins with statistics and ends with intuition — and on that account will probably satisfy nobody.

[2] Among the many lines of investigation traced in *The Structure of Spanish History* is the impingement of Arabic on Spanish, an impingement which Castro demonstrates going much deeper than lexicographical borrowing. Following Castro's lead, T. B. Irving, 'Completion and Becoming in the Spanish Verb', *Modern Languages Journal*, 1953, goes so far as to propose a full syntactical invasion of Arabic aspects into a number of Spanish constructions.

[3] *The New-Yorker*, May 15, 1954.

[4] I suspect that scholars who find epics in all sorts of non-civilized cultures use the term so loosely as to render it useless for literary criticism. The human and mortal heroism of the Occidental epic (from the *Iliad* to the great mediaeval poems) is a central exigency of the

which tenses could be anchored in sequence. Its technique of celebration resulted in freedom, freedom to introduce a new grammatical order, a way of expressing value that was alien to the time of the West.

Stephen Gilman

ı

genre affecting form and theme. As Lascelles Abercrombie shows (*The Epic, London*, 1914), without this basic definition of heroism, any kind of mythological or adventuresome poem (or motion picture) can be thought of as epic. As for the lack of epic in the Arabic world, Castro remarks: 'Furthermore, in Arabic literature the characters are dissolved in the narrated event, they are transformed into metaphorical expression or into moral wisdom; they never stand out "sculpturally" against other characters or against their environment. Neither characters or things have sharply chiselled existences. To feel the presence of a character presupposes feeling him as present and not as flowing through timeless time or unwinding in a continuous arabesque from one happening to another . . . Islam has no notion of existence in terms of a life that believes itself to be autonomous.' (*The Structure of Spanish History*, p. 287.) Hence, the lack of 'heroism' in the epic sense of the term. When Averroes, the great Arabic commentator and transmitter of Aristotle to the Western World, came to the *Poetics* his interpretation of the theory of tragedy and the tragic hero was highly inaccurate but still recognizable. For the epic, however, he broke down altogether: 'Aristotle describes the difference between the tragedy and the epic and explains which poets were best in each or which were unfortunate and unskillful and praises Homer above all the others. But this is a matter proper to the Greeks and among us there is not to be found anything of the sort either because [the epic] is not common to all people or because something supernatural has influenced the Arabs in this connection. The gentiles have in their "imitations" their own customs according to period and region.' I translate from the Spanish of Menéndez Pelayo who in turn translates from the Latin translation (*Historia de la ideas estéticas en España II*, Madrid, 1928, p. 154).

There are two aspects to the form of any work of literary art. In the first place, it is unique, a *techne* or artefact, to be examined by itself and without immediate reference to other things like it. In the second place, it is one of a class of similar forms. *Oedipus Rex* is in one sense not like any other tragedy, but it belongs to the class called tragedy. To understand what one tragedy is, therefore, leads us insensibly into the question of what an aspect of literature as a whole is. With this idea of the external relations of a form, two considerations in criticism become important: convention and genre.

The central principle of orthodox or Aristotelian criticism is that a poem is an imitation, the basis of imitation being, according to the *Physics*, nature. This principle, though a perfectly sound one, is still a principle which isolates the individual poem. And it is clear that any poem may be examined, not only as an imitation of nature, but as an imitation of other poems. Virgil discovered, according to Pope, that following nature was ultimately the same thing as following Homer. Once we think of a poem in relation to other poems, we begin to develop a criticism based on that aspect of symbolism which relates poems to one another, choosing, as its main field of operations, conventional or recurring images.

All art is equally conventionalized, but we do not ordinarily notice this unless we are unaccustomed to the convention. In our day the conventional element in literature is elaborately disguised by a law of copyright pretending that every work of art is an invention distinctive enough to be patented. To demonstrate the debt of A to B may get C his doctorate if A is dead, but may land him in a libel suit if A is alive. This state of things makes it difficult to appraise a literature which includes Chaucer, much of whose poetry is translated or paraphrased from others; Shakespeare, whose plays sometimes follow their sources almost verbatim; and Milton, who asked for nothing better than to copy as much as possible out of the Bible. It is not only the inexperienced reader who looks for a *residual* originality in such works: most of us tend to think of a poet's real achievement as distinct from, or even contrasted with, the achievement present in what he stole. But the central greatness of, for instance, *Paradise Regained* is not the greatness of the rhetorical decorations that Milton added to his source, but the greatness of the theme itself, which Milton *passes on* to the reader from his source.

The new poem, like the new baby, is born into an already existing order, and is typical of the structure of poetry which is ready to receive it. The notion that convention shows a lack of feeling, and that the poet attains 'sincerity' (which usually means articulate emotion) by disregarding it, is opposed to all the facts of literary experience and history. A serious study of literature soon shows that the real difference between the original and the imitative poet is that the former is more profoundly imitative. Originality returns to the origins of literature; radicalism returns to its roots. T. S. Eliot's remark that bad poets imitate and good poets steal affords a more balanced view of convention, as it indicates that the poem is specifically involved with other poems, not vaguely with such abstractions as tradition or style. The copyright law makes it difficult for a modern novelist to steal anything except his title from the rest of literature: hence it is often only in such titles as *For Whom the Bell Tolls* or *The Sound and the Fury* that we can clearly see how much impersonal dignity and richness of association an author gains by the communism of convention.

As with other products of divine activity, the father of a poem is much more difficult to identify than the mother. That the mother is always nature, the objective considered as a field of communication, no serious criticism can ever deny. But as long as the father of a poem is assumed to be the poet himself, we fail to distinguish literature from discursive verbal structures. The discursive writer as an act of conscious will, and that conscious will, along with the symbolic system he employs for it, is set over against the body of things he is describing. But the poet, who writes creatively rather than deliberately, is not the father of his poem; he is at best a midwife, or, more accurately still, the womb of Mother Nature herself: her privates he, so to speak. The true father or shaping spirit of the poem is the form of the poem itself, and this form is a manifestation of the universal spirit of poetry, the 'onlie begetter' of Shakespeare's sonnets who was not Shakespeare himself, much less that depressing ghost Mr. W. H., but Shakespeare's subject, the master-mistress of his passion. When a poet speaks of the *internal* spirit which shapes the poem, he is apt to drop the traditional appeal to female Muses and think of himself as in a feminine, or at least receptive, relation to some god or lord, whether Apollo, Dionysus, Eros, Christ, or (as in Milton) the Holy Spirit. Est *deus* in nobis, Ovid says: in modern times we may compare Nietzsche's remarks about his inspiration in *Ecce Homo*.

The problem of convention is the problem of how art can be communicable. Poetry, taken as a whole, is not simply an aggregate of artefacts imitating nature, but one of the activities of human artifice taken as a whole. If we may use the word 'civilization' for this, we may postulate a phase of criticism which looks at poetry as one of the techniques of civilization. It is concerned, therefore, with the social aspect of poetry, with poetry as the focus of a community.

The symbol in this phase is the communicable unit, to which I give the name archetype: that is, a typical or recurring image. I mean by an archetype a symbol which connects one poem with another and so helps to unify and integrate our literary experience. By the study of conventions and genres, it attempts to fit poems into the body of poetry as a whole.

The repetition of certain common images of physical nature like the sea or the forest in a large number of poems cannot in itself be called even 'coincidence', which is the name we give to a piece of design when we cannot find a use for it. But it does indicate a certain unity in the nature that poetry imitates. And when pastoral images are deliberately employed in *Lycidas*, for instance, merely because they are conventional, we can see that the convention of the pastoral makes us assimilate these images to other parts of literature. *Lycidas* leads us immediately to the whole pastoral tradition from Theocritus and Virgil down through Spenser and Milton himself to Shelley, Arnold and Whitman, and extends into the pastoral symbolism of the Bible, of Shakespeare's forest comedies, and so on endlessly. We can get a whole literary education simply by picking up one conventional poem and following its archetypes as they stretch out into the rest of literature. And if we do not accept this archetypal element in the imagery linking different poems together, it seems to me impossible to get any systematic mental training out of the study of literature alone.

The conception of copyright extends to a general unwillingness on the part of authors of the copyright age to have their imagery studied conventionally. In dealing with this period, many archetypes have to be established by critical inspection alone. To give a random example, one very common convention of the nineteenth-century novel is the use of two heroines, one dark and one light. The dark one is as a rule passionate, haughty, plain, foreign or Jewish, and in some way associated with the undesirable or with some kind of forbidden fruit like incest. When the two are involved with the same hero, the plot usually has to get rid of the dark one or make her into a sister if the story is to end happily. Examples include *Ivanhoe, The Last of the Mohicans, The Woman in White, Ligeia, Pierre* (a tragedy because the hero chooses the dark girl, who is also his sister) *The Marble Faun,* and countless incidental treatments. A male version forms the symbolic basis of *Wuthering Heights.* This device is as much convention as Milton's calling Edward King by a name out of Virgil's *Eclogues,* but it shows a confused, or, as we say, 'unconscious' approach to conventions.

An archetype is not a simple but a variable convention. Archetypes are associative clusters, and include a large number of specific learned associations which are communicable because a large number of people within a culture happen to be familiar with them. When we speak of symbolism in ordinary life we usually think of such learned cultural archetypes as the cross or the crown, or of conventional associations, as of white with purity or green with jealousy. Such archetypes differ from signs in being complex variables: as an archetype, green may symbolize hope or vegetable nature or a go sign in traffic or Irish patriotism as easily as jealousy, but the word green as a verbal sign always refers to a certain colour. The resistance of modern writers to having their archetypes 'spotted', so to speak, is partly due to a natural anxiety to keep them as versatile as possible, not pinned down exclusively to one interpretation, a practice which would allegorize their work into a set of esoteric signs.

At one extreme of literature we have the pure convention, which a poet uses merely because it has often been used before in the same way. This is most frequent in naive poetry, in the fixed epithets and phrase-tags of medieval romance and ballad, in the invariable plots and character types of naive drama. At the other extreme we have the pure variable, where there is a deliberate attempt at novelty or unfamiliarity, and consequently a disguising or complicating of archetypes. This last is closely connected with a distrust of communication itself as a function of litera-ture, such as appears in some forms of dadaism. It is clear that archetypes are most easily studied in highly conventionalized literature; that is, for the most part, naive, primitive and popular literature. In suggesting the possibility of archetypal criticism, then, I am suggesting the possibility of extending the kind of comparative study now made of folk tales and ballads into the rest of literature. This should be more easily conceivable now that it is no longer fashionable to mark off popular and primitive literature from ordinary literature as sharply as we used to do.

In the general Aristotelian or neo-Classical view of poetry, as expounded for instance by Sidney, the events of poetry are examples and its ideas precepts. (The vagaries of English make 'exemplary' the adjective for both words.) In the exemplary event there is an element of *recurrence,* something that happens time and again; in the precept, or statement about what ought to be, there is a strong element of *desire.* These elements of recurrence and desire come into the foreground in archetypal criticism. From this point of view, the narrative aspect of literature is a recurrent act of symbolic communication: in other words a ritual. Narrative (Aristotle's *mythos*) is studied by the archetypal critic as ritual or imitation of significant human action as a whole, and not simply as a *mimesis praxeos* or imitation of *an* action. Similarly, in archetypal criticism the significant content (Aristotle's *dianoia* or 'thought') takes the form of the conflict of desire and reality which has for its basis the work of the dream.

The union of ritual and dream in a form of verbal communication is usually called myth. The myth accounts for, and makes communicable, the ritual and the dream. Ritual, by itself, cannot account for itself: it is pre-logical, pre-verbal, and in a sense pre-human. Myth is distinctively human, as the most intelligent partridge cannot tell even the absurdest story explaining why it drums in the mating season. Similarly, the dream, by itself, is a system of cryptic allusions to the dreamer's own life, not fully understood by him, or so far as we know of any real use to him. But in all dreams there is a mythical element which has a power of independent communication, as is obvious, not only in the stock example of Oedipus, but in any collection of folk tales.

We may see two aspects of myth: structural or narrative myths with a ritual content, and modal or emblematic myths with a dream content. The former are most easily seen in drama: not so much in the drama of the educated audience and the settled theatre as in naive or spectacular drama: in the folk play, the puppet show, the pantomime, the farce, the pageant, and their descendants in masque, comic opera, commercial movie and revue. Modal myths are best studied in naive romance, which includes the folk tales and fairy tales that are so closely related to dreams of wonderful wishes coming true, and to nightmares of ogres and witches. The close relation of romance to ritual can be seen in the number of medieval romances that are linked to some part of the calendar, the winter solstice, a May morning, or a saint's eve. The fact that the archetype is primarily a *communicable* symbol accounts for the ease with which ballads and folk tales and mimes travel through the world, like so many of their heroes, over all barriers of language and culture. We come back here to the basis of archetypal criticism in primitive and popular literature.

By these words I mean possessing the ability to communicate in time and space respectively. Otherwise they mean much the same thing. Popular art is normally decried as vulgar by the cultivated people of its time; then it loses favour with its original audience as a new generation grows up; then it begins to merge into the softer lighting of 'quaint', and cultivated people become interested in it; and finally it begins to take on the archaic dignity of the primitive. This sense of the archaic recurs whenever we find great art using popular forms, as Shakespeare does in his last period, or as the Bible does when it ends in a fairy tale about a damsel in distress, a hero killing dragons, a wicked witch, and a wonderful city glittering with jewels. In fact archaism is a regular feature of all social uses of archetypes. Soviet Russia is very proud of its production of tractors, but it will be some time before the tractor replaces the sickle on the Soviet flag.

As the archetypal critic is concerned with ritual and dream, it is likely that he would find much of interest in the work done by contemporary anthropology in ritual, and by contemporary psychology in dreams. Specifically, the work done on the ritual basis of naive drama in Frazer's *Golden Bough*, and the work done on the dream basis of naive romance by Jung and the Jungians, are of most direct value to him. But the three subjects of anthropology, psychology and literary criticism are not yet clearly separated. *The Golden Bough* has had perhaps even more influence in literary criticism than in anthropology, and it may yet prove to be really a work of literary criticism. From the literary point of view, *The Golden Bough* is an essay on the ritual content of naive drama: it reconstructs an archetypal ritual from which the structural and generic principles of drama may be *logically*, not chronologically, derived. To the critic the archetypal ritual is hypothesis, not history. It is very probable that Frazer's hypothetical ritual would have many and striking analogies to actual rituals, and collecting such analogies is part of his argument. But an analogy is not necessarily a source, an influence, a cause or an embryonic form, much less an identity. The *literary* relation of ritual to drama is a relation of content to form, not of source to derivation.

The work of the Classical scholars who have followed Frazer's lead has produced a general theory of the spectacular or ritual content of Greek drama. But if the ritual pattern is in the plays, the critic need not take sides in the quite separate historical controversy over the ritual *origin* of Greek drama. It is on the other hand a matter of simple observation that the action of *Iphigeneia in Tauris,* for example, is concerned with human sacrifice. Ritual, as the content of action, and more particularly of dramatic action, is something continuously latent in the order of words, and is quite independent of direct influence. Rituals of human sacrifice were not common in Victorian England, but the instant Victorian drama becomes primitive and popular, as it does in *The Mikado,* back comes all Frazer's apparatus, the king's son, the mock sacrifice, the analogy with the Sacaea, and the rest of it. It comes back because it is still the primitive and popular way of holding an audience's attention, and the experienced dramatist knows it.

The prestige of documentary criticism, which deals entirely with sources and historical transmission, has misled archetypal critics into feeling that all ritual elements ought to be traced directly, like the lineage of royalty, as far back as a willing suspension of disbelief will allow. The vast chronological gaps resulting are sometimes bridged by a dubious conspiratorial theory of history involving secrets jealously guarded for centuries by esoteric cults. It is curious that when archetypal critics insist on continuous tradition they almost invariably produce some hypothesis of degeneration from a golden age lost in antiquity. Thus the prelude to Thomas Mann's Joseph series traces back several of our central myths to Atlantis, Atlantis being tolerable perhaps as an archetypal idea, but hardly as a historical one. When archetypal criticism revived in the nineteenth century with a vogue for sun myths, an attempt was made to ridicule it by proving that Napoleon was a sun myth. The ridicule is effective only against the historical distortion of the method. Archetypally, we turn Napoleon into a sun myth whenever we speak of the rise of his career, the zenith of his fame, or the eclipse of his fortunes.

Social and cultural history, which is anthropology in an extended sense, will always be a part of the context of criticism, and the more clearly the anthropological and the critical treatments of ritual are distinguished, the more beneficial their influence on each other will be. The same is true of the relation of psychology to criticism. Biography will always be a part of criticism, and the biographer will naturally be interested in his subject's poetry as a personal document, an interest which may take him into psychology. I am speaking here of the serious studies which are technically competent both in psychology and in criticism, which are aware how much guesswork is involved and how tentative all the conclusions must be. I am not speaking of the silly ones, which simply project the author's own erotica, in a rationalized clinical disguise, on his victim.

Such an approach is easiest and most rewarding with, say, Romantic poets, where the poet's own mental processes are often part of the theme. With a dramatist, who knows so well that 'They who live to please must please to live', there is greater danger of making an unreal abstraction of the poet from his literary community. Suppose a critic finds that a certain pattern is repeated time and again in the plays of Shakespeare. If Shakespeare is unique or anomalous, or even exceptional, in using this pattern, the reason for his use of it may be at least partly psychological. But if we can find the same pattern in half a dozen of his contemporaries, we clearly have to allow for convention. And if we find it in a dozen dramatists of different ages and cultures, we have to allow for genre, for the structural requirements of drama itself.

A psychologist examining a poem will tend to see in it what he sees in the dream, a mixture of latent and manifest content. For the literary critic the manifest content of the poem is its form, hence its latent content becomes simply its actual content or theme, Aristotle's *dianoia*. And in archetypal criticism the significant content of a poem is, we said, a dream. We seem to be going around in a circle, but not quite. For the critic, a problem appears which does not exist for a *purely* psychological analysis, the problem of communicable latent content, of intelligible dream. For the psychologist all dream symbols are private ones, interpreted by the personal life of the dreamer; for the critic there is no such thing as private symbolism, or, if there is, it is his job to make sure that it does not remain so.

This problem is already present in Freud's treatment of *Oedipus Rex* as a play which owes much of its power to the fact that it dramatizes the Oedipus complex. The dramatic and psychological elements can be linked without any reference to the personal life of Sophocles. The emphasis on impersonal content was developed by the Jungians, where the communicability of archetypes is accounted for by a theory of a collective unconscious—an unnecessary hypothesis in criticism, so far as I can judge. Now the poet, as distinct from the discursive writer, intends to write a poem, not to say something, hence he constructs a verbal pattern with, perhaps, millions of implications in it, of which he cannot be individually conscious. And what is true of the poet's intention is equally true of the audience's attention: their conscious awareness can take in only a very few details of the complex of response. This state of things enabled Tennyson, for instance, to be praised for the chastity of his language and read for his powerful erotic sensuousness. It also makes it possible for a contemporary critic to draw on the fullest resources of modern knowledge in explicating a work of art without any real fear of anachronism.

For instance, Le Malade Imaginaire is a play about a man who, in seventeenth-century terms, including no doubt Moliere's own terms, was not really sick but just thought he was. A modern critic may object that life is not so simple: that it is perfectly possible for a malade imaginaire to be a malade veritable, and that what is wrong with Argan is an unwillingness to see his children grow up, an infantile regression which his wife—his second wife, incidentally—shows that she understands completely by coddling him and murmuring such phrases as 'pauvre petit fils'. Such a critic would find the clue to Argan's whole behaviour in his unguarded remark after the scene with the little girl Louison (the erotic nature of which the critic would also notice): 'Il n'y a plus d'enfants.' Such a reading, whether right or wrong, keeps entirely to Moliere's text, and has nothing to do with Moliere himself.

Nor does it confine itself simply to the meaning of the play, but throws light on its narrative structure as well. The play is generically a comedy; it must therefore end happily; Argan must therefore be brought to see some reason; his wife, whose dramatic function it is to keep him within his obsession, must therefore be exposed as inimical to him. The movement of the play is exactly as logical and coherent as its total meaning, for the reason that they are the same thing, just as a piece of music is the same whether we listen to its performance or study its score. But, archetypally, the plot is a ritual moving through a scapegoat rejection to the prospect of marriage which is the normal end of comedy, and the theme is a dream-pattern of irrational desire in conflict with reality. The archetypal is only one of many possible critical approaches, and in the case of a highly civilized comedy of seventeenth-century France it may seem a somewhat peripheral one. But it gives us an insight into the structural principles of literature that we can get in no other way, as well as a clearer understanding of literature as a technique of communication.

Northrop Frye

Memorandum: To All TIME INC. Bureaus and Stringers

The big news in the art world today is the suddenly intensified row over the artistic merits of abstract, unintelligible art. It is indicative of a spreading revolt against 'extreme modernism'. More and more artists, both foreign and American, are beginning to shake loose from the grip of Picasso and other early modern leaders and to face up to reality in this chaotic period. The uprising is increasingly evident among critics, museum directors, dealers, and a general public exasperated with pictures requiring explanatory essays. The rebellion is concentrated in the U.S. which, through a sort of freak of economics, has become the art centre of the world. As such, the country is still contorted by a welter of conflicting native and foreign influences. But these are churning toward some kind of climax and order. In other words, the U.S. is struggling to assert itself and to evolve an art of its own, as it has at times in the past. This Battle for Art, with its background, manifestations, and dramatic developments, is ripe for solid, dynamic reporting.

In reporting on contemporary art we would like to follow this Battle for Art theme fairly consistently. Since executing it depends largely on a full and steady flow of information from the field, *anything at all pertinent* to the growing controversy between the proponents and antagonists of 'modern art' (unintelligible or otherwise) will be exceedingly welcome any time. The area of combat is quite broad, ranging from the public itself to directors of museums, critics, collectors, artists and so on. This memo does not mean that we are no longer interested in art story ideas unrelated to the Battle for Art. We are always in the market for any interesting story that comes your way. This memorandum describes briefly the background of the struggle and *Life's* editorial hopes as to its outcome. It also describes *Life's* reporting objectives and the story types we are looking for that ought to serve as a specific reportorial guide.

The revolt against unintelligible modernism was dramatically set off in Boston, that historic seat of rebellion. There the Institute of Modern Art suddenly announced early this year that it had changed its name to the Institute of Contemporary Art. The word 'modern', explained the Institute bluntly, connotes a 'general cult of bewilderment—rested on the hazardous foundations of obscurity and negation—utilizing a private, often secret language which required the aid of an interpreter—an attractive playground for double talk, opportunism and chicanery at the public expense'. The manifesto urged the artist to 'form closer ties' with a mystified, irritated public and cease to 'take refuge in private cynicism'. Thereafter the Institute would endorse only work that was at least intelligible. Enraged by the statement, a group of artists assembled in the Old South Meeting House and cut loose with a fiery counterattack. The Institute's condemnation, they said, was 'an invitation to reaction'. It discredited progressiveness, experimentation, and has perpetrated a 'serious harm to modern art, collectors of modern art and, primarily, to the freedom of expressive creation'.

The outburst uncorked a pent-up struggle that had been simmering for about thirty years over about every form of art that has come to be known loosely as 'modern'. Signs of the disturbance have struck the country with impartiality. They vary from outright denunciations by both sides, to actual splits within museums, artists' groups, etc., to the gradual, less spectacular changes in artists' works. In Des Moines, Iowa, the citizens are feuding over the question: what kind of art to hang in the city's brand new $700,000 museum? The Board of Trustees wants to fill it with conservative work. Assorted groups of artists and critics prefer middle-of-the-road painting; others, the modern. The director of the museum stated his liberal viewpoint and was promptly fired. The fracas has stirred up the entire city and may even get to the courts. Meanwhile the museum, a splendid structure representing the last word in gallery design, remains dismally empty of purchases. Denver is also having its troubles. There the modernists and the traditionalists are squabbling mightily, referring to each other respectively as radical and freakish or as amateurish Sunday painters. The modernists have just stalked out of the city's conservative Artists' Guild and have set up their own separate organization.

It is not surprising that the first angry sounds of revolt should emanate from a museum. A museum, after all, is often run as a business, and modern art, though it attracts curious, befuddled crowds, sells only to a small clique of devotees and to occasional snobs who think that realism is vulgar. But ever since the war, the revolt has been quietly, surely spreading among artists—and young ones in particular—who have found that total abstractionism is a frustrating, academic medium. Frank Wallace, for instance, who recently had his first one-man show at the Norlyst Gallery in New York, was painting Braquish and Mondrianesque abstractions two years ago. 'These', he said, 'were purely for the effect of nice design.' Now, he has just finished a series of paintings recognizable as Vermont landscapes, and is on his way to Italy to study the Old Masters. The war profoundly inspired many young painters to shift toward reality. Edward Melcarth, one of the ablest, has refused to retreat again into what he calls 'a technical world of matiere, mathematics and mysticism', and has turned out some powerfully realistic scenes of the effects of war. Several artists, Aronson, Green, Nordfeldt, Kopf, have created a stir among the critics by breaking from Picassoism and turning to religious subjects as a medium for expressing the tragedies and the hopes of today. To them straight abstractionism now seems a frivolous formula. Their work bears the influence of the early Renaissance, but it is more meaningful and individualistic than ever before. Raymond Beinin, well-known for his escapist fantasies, has turned to religious themes and portraiture. 'We have drifted away from the element of warmth between the artist and the subject', he explains, 'I draw very little inspiration from the cold, calculated *"isms"* of today—I am thinking in terms of portraiture because one cannot generalize the physiognomy of individuals—.' The famous painter Maurice Stern observes that too much art has sprung fully armed from the head of a Picasso, or a Braque or a Rouault.

The revolt is not by any means confined to artists in this country. In France, painters are talking loudly of a 'New Reality'; in Italy the rage is a 'New Humanism' which is particularly evident in beautifully sensitive, realistic sculpture. And some of the latest paintings of Braque reveal that even he is veering toward representational forms. More remarkable is the case of the famous Italian, Chirico, who has violently discarded his strange surrealist world and now paints like a realist.

What kind of art will emerge from the struggle in the U.S.? Now and then in the past the country has produced work of an essentially American character: the uncompromising realism of the 18th Century primitives and of John Singleton Copley's portraits which excited even the sedate London Academy; the peaceful grandeur of the Hudson River scenes; the tough genre reporting of the Ashcan Group (Sloan's *McSorley's Bar,* Bellow's *Dempsey-Sharkey Fight*) and finally the work of the American Scenists ranging from the careful touches of Grant Wood to Benton's bawdy, tobacco-chewing parables. The country is' artistically immature, but potentially it is powerful, lusty—and it is growing up. 'Watch the surge toward beauty', cried A. M. Frankfurter, 'real beauty, not the fascination of anecdote, nor the spell of eclecticism—.' It is to be hoped that Mr. Frankfurter is right. It is also to be hoped that the new art, which will no doubt retain a healthy stamp of modernism, will not resort to mere intellectual, occasionally decorative exercises, that it will not wallow in symbols of despair and escapism, but that somehow it will state the confidence and the robustness of the country. So far, the trend is right.

In many ways, the greatest shift in the way of conceiving knowledge between the ancient and the modern world takes place in the movement from a pole where knowledge is conceived of in terms of discourse and hearing and persons, to one where it is conceived of in terms of observation and sight and objects. This shift dominates all others in Western intellectual history, and as compared to it, the supposed shift from a deductive to an inductive method pales into insignificance. For the coming into prominence of deduction, which must be thought of in terms of visual, not auditory, analogies—the 'drawing' of conclusions, not the 'hearing' of a master—is already a shift toward the visual and a preparatory step for induction. Stress on induction follows the stress on deduction as manifesting a still further visualization in the approach to knowledge, with tactics based on 'observation', an approach preferably through sight.

The remote origins of the auditory-to-visual shift have been traced to the difference between the Hebraic concept of knowledge, auditory and consequently personalist and existential, and the Greek concept, based on analogy with vision. For the Hebraic, and perhaps for the present-day Arabic world, to know (*yadha'*) meant to know one's way around, to 'know what's what', to 'be in the know', whereas for the Greek, to know ($\gamma\iota\gamma\nu\acute{\omega}\sigma\kappa\omega$) meant to see, to intuit, to envision intellectually.

However, compared to the modern world, even the Greek tended to set knowledge within an auditory frame. Only with the slow development of scientism out of the Greek tradition have the promises or possibilities latent in the visualist orientation of the term $\gamma\iota\gamma\nu\acute{\omega}\sigma\kappa\omega$ been finally realized. Socrates' technique, if not his objective, had been real, oral dialogue. Plato retained this dialogue perforce in reporting Socrates' teaching but he reduced it to the visualist medium of writing and, in his own mind, allowed concern for dialogue to be eclipsed by the visualist notion which obsessed him, that of the 'idea' a term used originally to designate the look or appearance of things. Following Plato came Aristotle's search for 'objective' sciences—objects being items in a visile's universe, as persons are in an audile's.

Even Aristotle, who thought of himself as the inventor of logic, was far from decisive in dissociating this science from dialectic, that is, from implication with dialogue and sound. He used the term $\lambda o\gamma\iota\kappa\acute{\eta}$ to refer to dialectical reasoning, with its suggestion of dialogue, and generally equated $\lambda o\gamma\iota\kappa\tilde{\omega}s$ and $\delta\iota\alpha\lambda\epsilon\kappa\tau\iota\kappa\tilde{\omega}s$, contrasting both with the term $\dot{\alpha}\nu\alpha\lambda\upsilon\tau\iota\kappa\tilde{\omega}s$, which referred to scientific procedure, and with $\sigma\upsilon\lambda\lambda o\gamma\iota\sigma\mu\acute{o}$ which referred to formal reasoning or inference. Most significant of all, his notion of predication was based on 'saying' or vocal assertion; his categories or predicaments were radically things said of, or accusations brought vocally against, a subject.

This inability to dissociate an art of thinking from an art of speaking was passed on, directly or indirectly, through Cicero to the Middle Ages, and thence through John of Salisbury and, more equivocally, through Peter of Spain, until it floods into the Renaissance and crosses with other tendencies to generate curious offspring such as Ramism.

Compared to the ancient world, the world of scholasticism was a visualist age. The ancient educational ideal of the orator here yielded to a less auditory ideal as rhetoric was superceded by dialectic, and dialectic itself began to lose the two-sided character of genuine dialogue and attenuate itself into a teacher's monologue under the lecture system of the teachers' unions which we call universities.

Startling advances over Aristotelian logic were made in the medieval period by Peter of Spain, Ockham, Buridan, Burleigh, Tartaret, and others. As against Aristotle's logic, this medieval logic was, like modern mathematical logic, highly quantified, a logic with a high visual component.

91

One must keep in mind here an important fact: in the whole history of the human mind, mathematics and mathematical physics come into their own, in a way which changed the face of the earth, at only one time and place, that is, in Western Europe immediately after the scholastic experience. Elsewhere, no matter how advanced the culture on other scores, and even along mathematical lines, as in the case of the Babylonians, nothing like a real mathematical transformation of thinking has taken place—not among the ancient Egyptians or Assyrians or Greeks or Romans, not among the peoples of India nor the Chinese nor the Japanese, not among the Aztecs or Mayas, not in Islam despite the promising beginnings there, any more than among the Tartars or the Avars or the Turks. However great contributions other civilizations may hereafter make to the tradition, our scientific world traces its origins back always to 16th and 17th century Europe where for three centuries and more the arts course taught in universities and para-university schools had pounded into the heads of youth a study program consisting almost exclusively of a highly quantified logic and a companion physics, both taught on a scale and with an enthusiasm never approximated or even dreamt of in the ancient academies.

Sensitivity to space is obvious in the whole medieval, and even more the Renaissance, cultural complex, and is seen, for example, in the artist's attitude toward the world which he projected from his consciousness. 'Of all artists', remarks György Kepes, 'the Greeks alone reveal space concepts limited by Euclidean geometry.' With the Middle Ages, the artistic sensibility was already more spatially sophisticated, even when its relationship to the extended universe seemed more simple.

The mind had its spaces, too, and at the time of the Renaissance, nothing was more evident than the role which spatially oriented conceptualizations began to play in the notion of knowledge itself. The general stage had been set by the quantification of medieval logic, which gave occasion to think of mental operations less by analogy with hearing and more by analogy with spatial or geometric forms. The central operation in visualizing knowledge at this time was the exploitation of letterpress printing. I believe that there was an intimate connection between the mental habits encouraged by medieval logic and the emergence of printing. Basically, the new procedure gave permanence to sound by transmuting it more perfectly into silence, a technique for fixing the word in space more adroitly than ever before. Not only was it now possible to have an unlimited number of paper surfaces on each of which words were set in exactly the same spatial organization to one another, but the very technique of producing this spatial organization was itself an adventure in local motion which the parts of words had never seen before.

Writing had already reduced the sound of words to visual equivalents, or more accurately, visual distortions, and the alphabet had further dismembered these equivalents into visual parts. But printing from movable type cast from matrices struck from a die or punch—the essence of the achievement perfected by the Fust-Schöffer-Gutenberg combination—had spatially unmoored these parts themselves. Letters thus acquired local motion. More than that, their manufacture had been reduced to a matter of simple local manoeuvre. With one set of punches, one could move over bits of softer metal and strike out whole boxfuls of matrices. Casting from one set of matrices, one could produce whole fonts of type. With one font of type, one could set up an indefinite number of lines and compose an indefinite amount of type for making up an indefinite number of printing forms. From one form, one could print an indefinite number of pages simply by moving the paper into contact with the type and pressing it. Space had become pregnant with meaning, not only in the orderly arrangement within the book itself, but even more in the font of type, and still more in the little box of punches, in whose tiny compass were imprisoned more pagefuls of words than in a pre-Gutenberg inkwell the size of the Heidelberg tun.

This advance in the way of dealing with knowledge could not but affect the notions of what knowledge itself was. After the invention of printing, the notion of a book itself underwent immediate metamorphosis. Rather than a record of something someone had said, a book now became an object, belonging more to the world of things and less to the world of words. Silent reading began to replace the older oral habits of the manuscript age, when even a scholar reading privately to himself habitually picked the words off the page one by one and aloud. Book titles changed from addresses to the reader to labels, like those on boxes, for, with the spread of printing, books became items manufactured like tables and chairs. As objects or things, they obviously 'contained' knowledge. And, since knowledge could be 'contained' in books, why not in the mind as well?

At this point, the whole intellectual world goes hollow. The mind contains knowledge, especially in the compartments of the various arts and sciences, which in turn may 'contain' one another, and which all 'contain' words. Discourse contain sentences, sentences contain phrases, phrases words, and words themselves contain ideas. ('Sentences' or 'periods', 'commas', and the other paraphernalia of syntactical analysis were quite other things than this to ancient and medieval ban.) What is more, ideas contain other ideas.

The use of printing need not be regarded as the cause of this shift of the focus of knowledge toward spatial analogies, but rather as a spectacular symptom of the general reorientation going on. This reorientation is far flung in its implications, being connected on one side with the emergence of the topical or 'place'-logics; on another side with the interest in plotting the surface of the globe which makes this same Gutenberg era the great age of cartography and exploration; and on still another with the immeasurably greater exploitation today of visualist metaphors and of imagery which in one way or another admits of diagrammatic analysis.

The related visualist phenomena which appear in such riot are all, to a certain extent, subsumed or summarized in the changed way of conceptualizing the field of knowledge as a whole. The stepped-up visualism which reaches its initial climax in the Gutenberg era and thence moves on to still greater conquests was having consequences in man's way of picturing the universe of the mind quite as real as its consequences in man's way of thinking of the physical universe. No 'field' of knowledge was spoken of yet—that was to come later, as field physics was to come later, too—but the ways of thinking about mental activity had grown increasingly spatial in the Middle Ages.

One of the great climaxes in scholastic philosophy was the wave of interest in what we call today the 'structure' of a science (the term came into use in the late Renaissance period). By the late sixteenth century, this interest had become an obsession in the discussions on method and related matters which Ramus, Descartes, and Francis Bacon brought to a climax. Well before these men, the method discussions were big with diagrammatic symbols: 'method' itself (a 'way after' or 'way through'), *ascensus* and *descensus, analysis* and *synthesis* (a mathematical notion used by Ramists, and by others after them, to replace the more elusive, less diagrammatic *genesis* which had been the term Aristotle himself paired with *analysis*), and the like.

These concepts, derived from antiquity, basically are to be accounted for by the fact that attempts to explain mental activity tended to deal with the activity in terms of analogies with the sense of sight, since reduction in terms of one or another type of sense knowledge was inevitable, and reduction in terms of other senses, notably of hearing, while enhancing the mysterious and existentialist implications of knowledge, served little to satisfy the demand for some sort of explanation, for 'clarification'. However, despite their presence in philosophy from the beginning, nothing in antiquity or in the Middle Ages matched the clatter which such terms made from about the 1540's on. At Cambridge in the 1580's as at Paris three or four decades earlier, the method disputes threatened to set all the university dons and a great many of the students by the ears, first in the philosophy courses on the arts faculty, and thereafter by a kind of chain reaction up through the other faculties of medicine, law, and theology.

The notion of a philosophical 'system' or 'systems' is so well established today that it is hard for us to believe that it has a history at all. *Systema* is, of course, an ancient Greek term, translatable perhaps as 'set-up' or organized, composite whole, but its application to the realm of the mind, and in particular to philosophy, became current only after the medieval experience terminating in the methodological disputes, which gave unequivocal evidence of the penchant of the time for viewing knowledge with the help of visualist, quasi-diagrammatic constructs.

Conceived of as a 'way through' a problem or investigation, or as a 'way after' a desired answer, method is patently a concept based on a visualist analogy, which takes up the concept of 'way' and further visualizes it by conferring on it a fuller implication of direction. This fashion of dealing with the notion of 'way' contrasts strikingly with the Scriptural use of the term, where it occurs in obviously personalist and existentialist contexts: 'I am the way'—the 'I' being here not only a Person, but One to Whom the audile's rather than the visile's world is particularly relevant, the Incarnate Word of God, Who is also the Truth and the Life.

Walter J. Ong

In Eskimo the word to make poetry is the word to breathe; both are derivatives of *anerca,* the soul, that which is eternal, the breath of life. A poem is words infused with breath or spirit; 'Let me breathe of it', says the poet-maker and then begins: 'I have put my poem in order on the threshold of my tongue.'

Eskimos delight in recitation and the genius of their language, which is extremely expressive, full of onomatopoeic effects, favours it. Polysynthetic, indifferent to time, this language is the opposite of our analytic one with its preoccupation with lineality. Phrases are not composed of little words chronologically ordered, but of great, tight conglomerates, like twisted cables, within which concepts are juxtaposed and inseparably fused.

Suffixes are of major importance and affect only preceding parts, so that 'word' order is frequently the reverse of English:

1	2	3	4		4	3	2	1

nuna – tsia – ungi – tok means *It is – not – a nice – country.*

Thus a song duelist will begin with a great show of modesty and praise, then gradually unmask his fire by subtly modifying the suffixes of his opponent's name or habits, until the crowd collapses at a particularly adept play on words.

Questions philosophical are of little interest, at least in any abstract sense, for both hunters and wives are so absorbed in the immediate machinery of life that, perhaps fortunately, they can't really fix their undivided attention on cosmic mysteries. But they love to reflect on their language and if questioned on the etymology of a word, will give a variety of cocksure explanations, usually remarkably clever, but as often wrong. Anthropologists working with texts have learned to their sorrow that Eskimos are poets, not linguists. Ohnainewk, an Aivilik hunter, considered linguistic problems with quiet interest and volunteered explanations so novel and tantalizing I pursued each. Almost always he was wrong.

But then, just what do we mean by 'wrong'? The idea that a word has a fixed, single meaning he would deny. Like Humpty-Dumpty, he used words to mean exactly what he wanted them to mean, neither more nor less. And this, not with loose indifference, but with a precision of which he was both aware and proud. Without dictionaries to contradict him, he was a free agent with words, creating them with suffixes, combining them in new ways. The phrases he used were age old, at their simplest somewhat rubbed and worn repetitions of forms that had stirred the imagination and feeling of generations. The same statement goes for both the music and dancing associated with his poetry. There was an accepted vocabulary of tunes and movements of which, in the case of several, he was the identifiable 'owner'. But his poetry was often of a fresh, creative order. His art lay in giving these traditions new life by improvisations upon them, but not departing from (not destroying) the language itself. He was a composer, not merely a performer, a composer of variations upon known themes.

Disregarding chronology, he told stories in whatever order he chose. He usually began with the crisis, so to speak, and wove backwards and forwards in time, with many omissions and repetitions, on the tacit assumption that my mind moved in the same groove as his and that explanations were needless. By placing things side-by-side, not because they belonged there in time, but because they belonged there in his mind, he produced the most extraordinary effects—effects achieved only deliberately by some of our most sophisticated writers. By juxtaposing the seemingly incongruous, he arrested both ear and imagination; he set in motion new thoughts, and gave his poems life and depth. Life in the sense that he created new patterns, and in Eskimo thought, it is the non-lineal pattern which has value, not the sequence or causal relationship or comparison. Depth because each pattern incorporated the past, not as chronology or history, but as an ingredient, giving the pattern validity and value. Depth also through word plays (puns and word-linking), for nearly every poem hid an inspired, often indelicate, allusion whose riddle it took an adroit and practiced mind to unravel.

By beginning with the crisis, he was able to dwell on the nature of his own bravery or on his rival's treachery. For us the crisis comes at the end, as climax, and we arrange events and objects accordingly. Our mystery writers build up suspense, our movie reviewers take us up to the climax—but not beyond it, our humorists reserve the punch line for the end. But Ohnainewk was interested only in creating a living pattern and he took no care to follow a temporal sequence. On the contrary, he examined his subject first from here, then there, never pausing until he had achieved a multi-perspective which brought the subject to life. I stress all this, for unless we think of these poems as subtly constructed patterns, not stories narrated from the ground upward, we can never find the way to the Eskimo mind.

Of course, a good deal of Western poetry is not lineal either. But there is one important difference. Whereas with us such poetry is regarded by many as an unnatural and perverse way of distorting ordinary prose—worse still, a negation of 'disciplined thought'—in Eskimo society it is the normal and valued way of expression. Far from offering, as it does with us, 'another view', it reaffirms *the* view, that is, life. Language, mythology, dreams, values generally, all these are in harmony with it, and the poet finds no difficulty in communicating with his audience.

Frequently there is word continuity, especially in magical songs, where the key word in one line is caught in the next. Or the song duelist may take up his opponent's words. Or in interrogative poems, the whole question may be repeated in the answer, with the exception of the interrogative pronoun. This is more than just an effective stage trick: it's the crossing of one rhythm pattern with another. Here is the opening of Temmiartissaq's song at the consecration of her son's kayak:

kisim putuanin putuqarpoa	Whose claws have I for my claws?
cetonum putuanin putuqarpoa	The earwig's claws have I for my claws.
ke putuanik putuqarpoa	Whose claws have I myself for my claws?
ananana putuanik puturarpoa	The dung-fly's claws have I myself for my claws—

But such continuity is purely a product of poetic technique. There is only one Eskimo poem, known to me, which orders events lineally: the poem of the drowning raven. And the poet had little choice:

kesa tuwertiwaka tikitarpan	Now it reaches my great shoulders.
kesa taturtuara tikitarpan	Now it reaches my great chin.

98

kesa qanertiwara tikitarpan	Now it reaches my great mouth.
kesa qinartiwara tikitarpan	Now it reaches my great nose.
kesa takiwnatika tikitarpan	Now it reaches my great eyes.
rora (death-shriek)	Ugh!

Even poems which involve enumeration ignore lineality. A person is never described from head to toe, or a boat from bow to stern, or a life from birth to death, or an event from cause to consequence, or in any other fixed order. This enumeration is simply an assertion of power over the forces the poet calls by name, a magic formula. Exactness of pronunciation is the only essential element. No story is told, no sequential description given. In certain cases completeness of enumeration has cabalistic value; otherwise elements are added or dropped at will. Each is self-contained, discrete. Some have a kind of magic finality in themselves.

Such poems are not designed to *say* anything, but rather *to be said*. Their motifs are like moveable stage properties, appearing in a variety of contexts. Reason is not supreme, in control, with mind leading to statement and statement to action; 'information' is either absent or incidental, like words in music or pictorial representation in art. In many the thought content is only sufficient to hold the audience while the chant or incantation takes place; others are completely unhampered by thought. Eskimo poems, like Eskimo myths, are, I believe, essentially magical, ritualistic; satisfaction lies in the act of recitation, not in producing results or in influence or in projection. Their validity lies in their very being, in their proper performance, in their inheritance, in the realization of their mythical basis. True, some reflect the social structure, others contain models for action and judgement. But insofar as these intrude, value is absent or destroyed. The successful poet avoids such irrelevancies and simply gives himself over to the very stuff of his medium. His poetry is subservient neither to mind nor virtue, for these, however honorable, do not bring him any closer to the creative act, but separate him from it. Whatever they may do, they do not make Eskimo poetry and for the patent reason that this poetry does not come out of them but by its own, very different branch, from the human root itself.

Eskimo poems include petting songs and children's ditties, incantations, chants while hunting or paddling the kayak or while wandering in the hills picking berries, songs sung by the angakok when he calls his spirits, and dramatic and judicial drum-songs in which the singing and poetry unite with the solo dancing and the pounding, flowing rhythms of the drum to form a fugue-like composition.[1] Many of the first are meant to

[1] For the poems, translations, and text I have drawn very heavily from William Thalbitzer's *Meddelelser om Gronland*, Bind 40, and to a lesser extent from Svend Frederiksen's *Meddeleser om Gronland*, Bind 137:7; D. Jenness' *Songs of the Copper Eskimos;* and my own

be recited, not sung. The voice is not free or accidental, but bound to certain tonal movements, fixed by tradition, that produce a sort of word-melody. Incantations employ this musical speech, but with less variety in rhythms and tones. These are exceptions. No other poems occur without music and expressive movements, and most are accompanied by drumming.

At intervals during the winter the community collects in the dance house, the drum appears, and both sexes arrange themselves in a circle about the performer. Drumming and singing, he moves slowly round and round the circle, knees slightly bent, sometimes hopping lightly on both feet, more often moving them alternately, without any attempt to keep time with the drum-beats. The audience accompanies him in singing, but he remains largely independent of them, although he often tries to rouse them by increased vigour in his drumming and singing and by occasional whoops of joy. Sometimes he uses no drum at all, or hands it to one of the singers in the circle. Now he is more dependent on his audience for music, but his hands are free, and after awhile he ceases to sing and simply gesticulates violently, hopping and whooping with delight.

Poetry is not limited to such states of ecstasy. True, in the folktales, the lyric is reserved for emotional crises, moments for which prose is insufficient. But one hears poems and songs throughout the day: the old woman sewing, the hunter back from the kill, exactly mimicking the gait of the bear, the children catching lemmings. I watched a young couple courting: she would recite a verse, then shyly hide behind a rock; he would find her and reply—like kittens playing on the tundra.

Many of the drumsongs exhibit real craftmanship. Each stanza is composed of a burden and a refrain. The refrain, *tima*, 'the body', constitutes the bulk of the song which it opens and closes, often with an added derisive shout or a moaning yell last of all. Generally it contains one word of sense, namely a demonstrative pronoun, a word of direction, or a similar particle, but beyond that only one or two meaningless words which are repeated in varying forms. When using a word of direction, the poet may point with the drum, as if saying 'when I was up there' or 'this one here' (my opponent) or indefinitely, though passionately, 'Well, that's it! begin!' The term *aja* is repeated and varied as required by the melody (*e.g.*, *a·ja, aja·, ä·ja, ä·jai*, etc,) and once in awhile is superseded by *ara* or *aha* which are also varied. Many poems have no refrains and

---

field-work among the Aivilik. Thus the data come from several distant groups and are not applicable in every case; the elaborate song-duel, for example, is uniquely Greenlandic. But there is a basic unity which only a common tongue, common interests, and a common delight could foster, and for the points I wish to make here, I believe their joint treatment is justified. No attempt has been made, because of cost, to employ special phonetic symbols; for accurate recordings see Thalbitzer.

the stanza is generally, though not always, limited to drumsongs. Each singer has his own refrain-forms and the natives need only hear the refrain or part of it to recognize 'the owner'. The poet's drumsong is called his *pia*, his property, and it's considered unfair for another to sing or recite it as long as he lives. But a drum-singer may borrow a part of one of the songs of his forefathers and use it as an introduction in his own work. The refrain is repeated, almost unchanged, around each new burden in which the poet expresses 'what he has on his mind to say'. Here is a complete Ammassalik drumsong:

Refrain		Burden		Refrain
awnwaja ahaje	anɔa	akeagianenuanitaɹaja	jajaja	ajaiɔja ajaje
awnwaja ahaje	awnɔa	kenenuanitaɹaja	jajaja	ajaiɔa ajaje
awnwaja ahaje	awnɔa	tawaatenuataja	ajajaja	ajaiɔja ajaje
awnaja araje	awnɔa	akeanuɔnɔtaɹaja	ajajajai	ajaiɔja ajaje
awnaja araje	awnɔa	tawaatenuataja	ajajaja	ajaiɔja ajaje
awnwaja ahaje	awnɔa	ipinianɔtaaja	ajajaja	ajaiɔja ajaje
awnwaja araje	awnɔa	qamutsiaaluaniwaɹaja	ajajaja	ajaiɔja ajaje
awnwaja ahaje	(exclamation) e· ·a!	a hɔ·, a ha·, a ha!		

Whereas the refrain is unhampered by grammar or logic and hence easily brought under the yoke of rhythm, with the burden the poet has the problem of moulding language, for though flexible, it is limited to the forms prescribed by grammar. He does this partly by rhythm and partly by assonances and rhymes, though the last are rare. The innate rhythmics of the Eskimo words themselves produce metric cadences which are carried further by means of the polysynthetic power of the language. Iambi, trochees, dactyls, spondees and anapests vary in an inexhaustible stream. Regular metra are absent, but something approaching definite rhythmic types seems to have been evolving.

This is a highly conservative literature, moving through time and space with remarkably little change. It is kept alive, however, by the temperament of the speaker whose dynamic accent at all times acts as a recreating principle, constantly shifting the pronunciation of words, and subtly modifying meaning. The reciter has far greater freedom with pitch and stress than with words, and he makes full use of this license, especially in punning. Many are masters at recitation. They vary tempo, maintain intervals, melodiously raise and lower the voice to the extent of two or more notes, and adjust it to express emotions. Here are several Ammassalik poems:

pucepon   — — ◡
tacepon   — — ◡
amartaja   ◡ _́ ◡ ◡̀

sikartaja	⏑ $\acute{-}$ ⏑ $\grave{-}$
tinituin tara	⏑ $\acute{-}$ ⏑ ⏑ ⏑ $\acute{\smallsmile}$
aninacat	⏑ ⏑ $\acute{-}$ —
nunakacat	⏑ ⏑ $\acute{-}$ —
mana mana	$\acute{-}$ ⏑ $\acute{-}$ ⏑
suna mana	⏑ $\acute{-}$ $\acute{-}$ ⏑

1

A charm has this prosodial structure:

ea ea—	awaler	uiarpara
⏑ ⏑ | ⏑ ⏑ |	⏑ ⏑ —	⏑ ⏑ — ⏑ ⏑
⏑ ⏑ | ⏑ ⏑ |	⏑ ⏑ —	⏑ — ⏑ ⏑
⏑ ⏑ | ⏑ ⏑ | ⏑ ⏑ ⏑ ⏑		⏑ ⏑ — ⏑
	⏑ ⏑ ⏑ ⏑	⏑ ⏑ — ⏑
⏑ ⏑ | ⏑ ⏑ | — ⏑ ⏑		⏑ ⏑ — ⏑
	— ⏑ ⏑	⏑ ⏑ — ⏑
⏑ ⏑ | ⏑ ⏑ | — ⏑ ⏑		⏑ ⏑ — ⏑
	— ⏑ ⏑	⏑ ⏑ — ⏑

One curious effect—perhaps caused by consideration of a tabooed word —is achieved thus: *mana mana ajiwaitino*, 'But this here they are not good at', where 'this' (to sew) is shown by gesture.

But the principal effect is gained by repetition, particularly rhythmic repetition. A phrase is given, then repeated in another way, perhaps more emphatically, but always concisely. To this may be added final rhymes, *e.g.*, *aniwag / uwananiway*, and assonances or dissonances, *e.g.*, *at·ame irare··wa / ut·ume irare··wa*. Some of the longer poems are constructed so that either the same act is attempted by a number of people, one after another, or one person has a series of adventures which are described in exactly the same form. The story itself is incidental. Certainly the order in which incidents occur is interchangeable. To our ear and our taste, at least as adults, this rhythmic repetition is intolerably monotonous, but the Eskimos love it.

One remarkable poem completely misled me. I heard it from an Aivilik hunter who, laughing with delight, sang it as we walked across the tundra. First he related in prose the story of a man who had taken a wife against her will, fathered two children, and then abused her until she and the children left him. The poem begins when he sets out on a great Odyssey to find them. Other than the beginning, when he starts, and the end, when he finds them, there is nothing in the poem but a collection of ordeals the man is forced to undergo. Their order is of no consequence. Each incident is discrete, self-contained, and hence related in full. Where we might say, 'He proceeded northeast for so many miles, successively overcoming A, B, and C, until he reached his destination', the Aivilik neither plot course nor structure plot. Instead, they give each ordeal in full, even though it varies in only a few words from all the others. No effort is made to build up suspense; the ordeals do not become successively greater, nor does the hero gradually weaken. At first I thought the poem allegorical, depicting a series of temptations which the hero overcomes. But then I realized that the ordeals had nothing to do with temptations of the spirit or flesh, but were simply tests of physical prowess. Confronted with a pot of meat the size of a lake, he eats it all; when the lower half of a woman keeps blocking his path, he has intercourse until she is satisfied. Temptations of gluttony and sex are not overcome; they are indulged in. The Eskimos would really be impressed by a man who could drink a river dry.

During the extended nursing period, and especially when the infant is in the mother's parka, 'up there', an intimate language, often expressed in petting poems, develops between them. These are recited with a particular accent and pitch, but are devoid of real tones. Some are designed for special occasions, the naming rite perhaps, to instil in the child a certain vitality, but most are simply between mother and child. In the following one the infant is 'mother's sister', that is, identical with the person after whom she is named, for the deceased person's soul accompanies its name into the new-born child:

apina suka pinitsn	See her up there, the innocent coquette –
amiatanila	No man yet has touched her,
qumiatanila	No man yet has stamped her –
anananila	She is not my child's mother,
arqaliwanila	She is not my child's brother –
ajana	But she is mother's sister
qatanania	Crook-backed (as she was)
uteqiatan	Stammering
piteruatan	Restless in all her movements –
utanianiwa	From early morning wishing but to fall in with menfolk,
quatiwanianiwa	She tries to outwit them, the little creature –
ajaniwa	See how she raps with her hands,
qeaniwa	Hear how she whimpers –
awpalekuconoa	Hey! How she can run!

Half sung, half chanted in expressive melody, there are a number of little poems which mothers teach their children, or children one another:

ukuarpon　$\grave{\ }\ \smile\ \grave{\ }\ \diagup$　Our sister-in-law

ikarpon	‿ ˅ ⌐	Crosses the sound
qertamon	˅ ‿ ⌐	To the island
pomime	˅ ‿ ⌐	Why do you swim?
iwtimata	× ˅ × ⌐	You are well off
timane	‿ ˅ ⌐	On the firm land
itartite	˅ × ‿ ⌐	While you stand and laugh. –
natinarpu natinarpu natinarpoq		She is unhappy, unhappy, unhappy

10

While picking berries on the slope of the fell high above the settlement, a woman looks down at the kayaks on the sea and is overcome by her grief:

aliatagtiwa ia ia – –	Great grief came over me –
aliatagtiwa ia ia – –	Great grief came over me,
qartinilema nuniaqaliwa	While on the fell above us I was picking berries.
aliatagtiwa	Great grief overcame me
seqinertima nuilitara ia ia –	My sun quickly rose over it.
aliatagtiwa ia ia – –	Great grief came over me.
imartamana ia ia – –	The sea out there off our settlement
qatinalertiwaq ia ia –	Was beautifully quiet –
saqisiniwartiwit ia ia –	And the great, dear paddlers
autalersit	Were leaving out there –
aliatagtiwa ia ia – –	Great grief came over me
qartiniliwa nuniaqaliwa ia ia –	While I was picking berries on the fell.

Recited in private, interlarded with holy words, the magical chants and incantations range from 'cheap household remedies' to holy poems that are the very blood of the Eskimo. Refrains and stanzas are neither shouted, nor sung, nor whispered. The voice keeps a controlled tempo and medium strength, and a peculiarly impressive and mystic tone, as if the prayer were meant to be heard by one who is quite near and need not be summoned. There is a small group of poetical words and expressions, striking for their rhythms and tones. Some are sacred, taken from the ritual language, but they play no important part outside of poems with a religious character, which, however, make up a considerable portion of this unwritten literature. About them there is, as it were, a veil. No hypothesis, no science, can ever get fully in touch with that which the Eskimo feels when he lets himself sink into the meaning and sound of these words. They are symbols, not notions. In them is the centre of gravity of the Eskimo world view.

What appears to be metaphor here may be misleading. When a poet says, 'I breathe with the lung of the caterpillar and the bat' or 'I wish that the bat inside me might disappear', I do not think he is necessarily speaking metaphorically, but rather pointing out the participation of one thing in another. The qualities of the bat are to some extent *his own* ingredients, and since the word for bat and the bat itself are inseparable, parts of a single process, then employing the word for bat reminds him that he, in fact, partakes of bat-ness.

ea ea ake	Come hither,
tarnaka ake	My souls, come hither!
ea ea namine iwerte	Yourselves make ye fast!
tarnaka ime iwerte	My souls, of your own accord creep in!
ea ea pusaqiartino	Again slinking therein (?)!
ea ea tarnaka ake	My souls, come in!
ea ea ime iwerte	Of your own accord make ye fast
tarnaka ime iwerte	My souls, of your own accord creep in!
ea ea	

The angakok carries on conversations with the spirits he calls forth in poems. He is a ventriloquist—the voice comes now from the body, now from the deep into which his soul has subsided, now from the igloo ceiling. Then one, then another spirit is heard, singing songs of another type, which contain descriptions of their travels or accounts of their work in the priest's service. All are sung with long refrains and beating of drums, sometimes with the congregation joining the chorus in unison. Here is the song of Kukkujooq. Another woman has 'made her dark, internally' and the angakok has been summoned:

cilate ercinakajik	What on earth! I fear and tremble!
uwana ercinakajik	I fear and tremble on account of myself
takilwɔleqiwnana	That he will begin to look at me again.
iɹikasinajaqawna	Does he begin to make it out, he down there!
tarterujokajik	A great terrible darkness,
qernertertujokajik	A great terrible darkness,
ercikajik	Dreadful.

Two men, and sometimes two women, having become enemies, once a year give vent to their anger in poetical form, drumming and singing against each other. Their songs are often composed long before, carefully considered and rehearsed. The introduction may be borrowed from some old, well-known song, and the melodies and refrains may be inherited, but the burden is generally original. It is full of accusations, sneering references, innocent words with sinister meanings, and laments over the singer's own difficult position, his mean self—confessed with astonishing honesty and self-irony, perhaps to win the audience's sympathy. For the singers stand in the midst of a forum of critical listeners, whose verdict is laughter, and the aim of each poet is to have this laughter constantly directed toward his opponent. Much of the skill lies in tricks with words impossible to translate, and often a jest depends upon a custom or allusion with which a foreigner is unfamiliar. But the

Eskimo can translate the allusion or parry the thrust, and the highest form of verbal debate is to match a rival's series point for point. The poet begins by isolating an essential feature—Eskimos are gifted in picking nicknames which are always understood and usually extremely funny —then he will begin to play with this word, saying one thing, meaning another, innocent enough to common ears, but deadly with double meanings. One frequent form is to propound a question, appear astonished or indignant, and then immediately after answer it.

11

The songs are constantly renewed: the old are improved or replaced and favorites pass into popular tradition. Here is that latter half of an answering song:

natinartoruna	That poor being!
sujora napianejoqulin	Might his nose also be turned upwards!
sorto ilana	That gets me to think of
sujorartiwokaina	My own great, long nose,
pilatortiwokajik	A mighty, great knife,
pilatsiane	Please cut his nose in shape
kikitalanertino	And make it a knife with a notch
nuliane kaputisialono	For use when he stabs his wife.
ilanutimerakin	I was witness to your misdeed,
nulianeuwin	When your good little wife,
nukataneuwin	When your nice little 'young-sister wife',
iwtikaje kapilalikajenakin	When you scoundrel began to stab her again and again,
kapenernanewna	And you were not content with stabbing her,
ilimutu netuiartartino	No, you bored into her, inwards, incessantly,
putarqelusetaluoragin	Without preventing a swelling up like a seal bladder (?)
ilimuto netsortorpatarqawt	Inwards, you bored too long!
qujanaliwaqaq	It was only a very great fortune
nulianeupit	That your nice little wife
nukataneupit	That your nice little 'young sister'
pilawtat kiwikorilarimane	Sank your knife into the sea –
pulawta kiwiluat	Your knife, now sunk fortunately (?)

In the legend of Aaraattuaq, two enemies, having reviled each other in song through many years, at last become so used to it and so fond of it that they decide to continue their drum fighting after death. And then, when Aaraattuaq is the first to die and in his grave hears his opponent approach singing, calling him out, he rises from the stones of his grave and sings his drumsong on them, using his scapula as a drum and his fibula as a drumstick.

Edmund Carpenter

The relations between reality (*i.e.*, the total natural and man-made complex) and language are not constant but vary over the epochs. But within each epoch, defined by a certain state of consciousness, they are tolerably stable.

The relations of words and reality within an epoch are never neutral but either essentially affectionate or disaffectionate. This does not make it impossible for a writer living in an era of disaffection to establish an affectionate nexus (Wallace Stevens) or contrariwise (Swift). But such writers are not, strictly speaking, representative of their era: they are either late-comers or forerunners—expositors of a past state of consciousness or prophets of a state yet unrealized.

In an era of disaffection, the subjective tendency of language makes it pretend to equal status with the objective (*i.e.*, reified) character of reality. In individual experience as well as in the experience of the society so concerned, the Promethean pretension to equality will necessarily assume the colours of a bid for supremacy. It is the latter pretense—a quirk caused by a slight increase in self-consciousness and in its turn fostering a further and more drastic increase—which leads the writer to apprehensions of absurdity both in the universe and in the human mind.

There is nothing inherently absurd about man's disproportion to the rest of nature, including the world of tools and machines. Primitive men through the ages have felt both outnumbered and overpowered by non-human forces without entertaining such apprehensions. Absurdity is a matter of language: that alone is absurd which strikes the ear, and by extension the mind, discordantly. The oracle at Delphi and the Sphinx at Thebes are the first great sign-posts of absurdity in the history of the Western mind: the points at which awe—inspired by mere incomprehension of divine or daemonic speech—passes into temporary bemusement or discomfiture, caused by the sudden recognition of the equivocal aspect of language.

The growth of self-consciousness, once started, disallows either stoppage or reversal. So does language, its index, after passing through the univocal phase move irreversibly via the equivocal towards the multivocal. Since self-consciousness and language are as inseparable as current and meter, or indeed any process and the apparatus that registers it, the elucidation of language must keep step with the elucidation of mind as attempted by psychology and epistemology. In postulating that the process of self-consciousness be completed, we postulate the completion, *pari passu*, of the process of linguistic analysis.

But in our computations we must not forget the quirk mentioned earlier: the nisus of mind toward supremacy in the realm of nature; the element, as it might be called, of ontological illusion. The relation we are discussing partakes of that illusion and has done so since the dawn of history. That the illusion itself is wider in reference does not make it any the less integral to the issue. Every assumption of equality has supremacy as its $\tau\acute{\epsilon}\lambda os$; witness the Titans, the Olympian gods, Prometheus. To trace some of the stages of this necessary conversion—Homer, Hesiod; the Renaissance (Leonardo da Vinci); the Enlightenment (Bacon, Descartes, Hobbes)—has proved fruitful for the historian of ideas and the psychologist; it might prove so for the student of linguistics and semiotics as well. It can be shown with some plausibility that the Renaissance aimed consciously at equality only, the Enlightenment at supremacy. This spells, besides an advance in competence and scientific ingenuity, an advance in self-consciousness and, by the same token, in both articulateness and ambiguity of expression. Man's passage from a desire to steal nature's secrets to success (and consequent pride) in 'outwitting' her—the passage, in other words, from the scientific speculations of the early Renaissance to modern technology—is precipitated in so many linguistic counters which, though largely open to scrutiny, have so far received only sporadic examination. The process of history can never be comprehended in terms of plans and procedures alone, though plans and procedures are of the essence; nor in terms of subconscious motivations, now furthering now aborting men's plans and procedures—though these too are essential: another discipline is needed to complement what Marx, Freud and Weber have taught us about the norms as well as the vagaries of Western society. This discipline will be concerned not with man's conscious or unconscious acts but with his developing self-consciousness; and the study of self-consciousness is nothing other than the study of language or, more exactly, of the power (δύναμις) of language to deal with the reality man creates for himself in each period of history. This image of reality is never wholly a product of speech, as semanticists are fond of claiming; but neither has it remained independent of speech as some positivists assert, or engaged speech for purposes of rationalization only as most psychoanalysts would seem to suggest. Contrariwise, language, though not thoroughly 'real' partakes of the nature of objective reality; and so far from rising (or declining) towards the status of sheer instrumentality—in the sense of modern logic—it asserts its ontological status the more stubbornly, the more rudely our scrutiny tears layer after layer from its substance. Like his reality, then, man's language is neither an onion nor a bottomless pit: it is an infinite process, roughly determinate in each of its phases, and capable of adequate statement if the necessary pains are taken. The term 'adequate' hints at the limitation of all discourse; short of this there is no methodological objection to testing the self-consciousness of an age by the words it minted, banned, re-issued with new denominations, any more than to testing the consciousness of an age by what it did, or refused to do, or dissembled.

Francis Golffing

Twenty-three miles from Agra in India, with its fabled Taj Mahal, lies Fatehpur Sikri, a dream city built in sandstone the colours of the dying sunset. One approaches Fatehpur Sikri in silence, for it has been deserted for over two hundred years, but immediately on entering the core of the city—the Mahal-i-Khas—the heart is uplifted, the eye entranced. One experiences a rare sensation of freedom and repose—an invitation to step forward buoyantly and, at the same time, to loiter luxuriously. Wherever the eye turns the view is held, but at every step it changes. A seemingly solid background wall of stone is later perceived as a transparent screen. But nowhere is there a fixed centre: nowhere a point from which the observer can dominate the whole. Equally nowhere does he stand conspicuously removed from the centre—a spectator in the wings. From the moment he steps within this urban core he becomes an intimate part of the scene, which does not impose itself upon him, but discloses itself gradually to him, at his own pace and according to his own pleasure.

The Mahal-i-Khas was the core of a city of perhaps fifty thousand people. It is a place somewhat larger than the Piazza San Marco in Venice and, like it, is framed by buildings and openings, as well as having buildings standing within it as objects, both dimensioning its own space, and being set off by it. Despite un-Western details of architectural ornament, the contemporary visitor to Fatehpur Sikri is at once struck by the likeness of the spatial composition of these solids and voids in the Mahal-i-Khas with our modern Western thinking about the interplay of freedom and enclosure, transparency and repose.

Nothing in this deserted city of Fatehpur Sikri is fortuitous, and none of the effects are due either to the accretions of time, nor to its ravages. The city was built at one stroke by Akbar the Magnificent around 1570 and was deserted, but not destroyed, some twenty years later. Though many of the buildings themselves are very fine, the supreme quality of the Mahal-i-Khas lies in its superb proportioning of space. Most of the buildings within and around it are themselves symmetrical in their design, but their spatial setting is never axial. While it is clear at first glance that this is an ordered composition, one looks in vain for the key to it in terms of Western academic art. This article is an attempt to find that key.

It is very difficult for us to get away from the rules of the accepted vision of our Western culture and to realise, even intellectually, that this is not the only way of looking at things. For instance our eyes in the West have for five hundred years been conditioned, even governed, by another intellectual approach: the single viewpoint. This, though no more intellectual than the acceptance of the dominance of the vertical, is more readily grasped as an acquired characteristic of our vision. It is however peculiar to the western world where it followed the development of the science of optics: the study of the eye as an inanimate piece of mechanism pinned down upon the board of the scientist. The optical result was the development of linear perspective: the single 'vanishing point' and the penetration of landscape by a single piercing eye —my eye, my dominating eye. This created a revolution in our way of perceiving the objects around us, and in the rational organisation of landscape—whether rural or urban. The 'view' came into being: the penetration of infinity by means of a guided line—usually an avenue of trees or a symmetrical street. With this came the 'vista', the termination of the organised view by an object of interest, often the elaborately symmetrical facade of a large building, that could only be rightly beheld from a central point at some distance from it. All other views were, consciously and unconsciously, accepted as wrong: 'This is the place to see it from'.

For many it is extremely difficult, even uncomfortable, to accept linear perspective as a conditioned form of vision; limited and partial in its scope. 'That is exactly the way it looks to me' is the usual description of a good photograph, for the camera with its single fixed eye expresses linear perspective perfectly.

111

But the rest of the world sees things quite differently.

A Chinese painting is always presented to a spectator whose eye roves along a scroll or up a vertical painting. For instance, in a typical vertical painting of mountain scenery, the spectator will first find himself looking slightly down upon a cottage or fisherman at the foot of the picture —his eye perhaps on the level with the branches of a nearby pine tree. Then he will notice the ascending mountain path, but by now his eye will have moved, and he will be scanning the scenery from a higher vantage point. After a bit his moving eye will light upon a high mountain meadow, or other resting place, and from there, from that viewpoint, he will look up to the inaccessible peaks, half hidden in cloud. The spectator does not see an instantaneous picture of the entire mountain scene through the peephole of an imaginary camera in the cockpit of a helicopter hovering in mid-air; he participates, through his moving eye, in the inter-relationship of man and mountain. Similarly, on the long scroll paintings, the eye moves slowly into the picture from the right, the scene always changing, always unfolding. Objects come more usually towards the spectator than recede from him, for here the eye seldom pierces the landscape. The technique of drawing is a form of parallel perspective rather than linear perspective: the spectator usually being at an angle to the scene (rather than the focus of it) and parallel lines often slightly opening as they recede—emphasising his ever central but ever moving position.

This changing vision, this absence of the restraining blinkers of the single viewpoint, existed in our Western world in classical times. A typical example can be seen in some of the wall paintings, now in the Metropolitan Museum of New York, taken from the room of a house in Boscoreale in Southern Italy around the opening of the Christian era. An elaborate urban scene is depicted: buildings of several stories, with projecting balconies and long colonnades, rise one behind the other. There are courtyards, trees, steps, and streets. The spectator grasps the scene from a series of viewpoints, floating about somewhere in front of it, his eye now beneath an overhanging balcony, now above a projecting roof. But each 'eye-full', each object upon which his eye momentarily rests, is drawn, as we might say, 'correctly'.

In a thesis that I have not read, a Greek scholar, Dr. C. A. Doxiades, attempts an explanation of the asymmetric, but certainly carefully planned, disposition of the buildings on the Acropolis at Athens. He represents the field of vision of the eye as an equilateral triangle—with the eye and not the vanishing point as the apex. He then places this human eye at a series of vantage points upon the Acropolis, and demonstrates how, from each of these visual stopping places, the eye was presented with a completely organised and balanced architectural scene.

112

With these examples in mind one can again approach Fatehpur Sikri to see whether they offer us some help in trying to solve the system of thought that underlay its highly intellectual, highly organised and subtle composition that gives the spectator such a sensation of ease and delight.

There are several fairly obvious resting places within the Mahal-i-Khas, the most notable being perhaps the roof of Akbar's private appartments, the terraces of the Panch Mahal (the 5-storied Pleasure Pavilion), the entrance to the Dewan-i-Khas (the Hall of Private Audience) and the balcony overlooking the great outer court, the Dewan-i-Am (Hall of Public Audience). From each of these stations one is presented with a carefully balanced panoramic scene: not with a central objective it is true, but with a single co-ordinated sweep of vision or 'eyefull'. In each of these cases, the scene has a transparent centre and equivalent, but not identical, objects of interest bounding the view to right and left. For instance, from the entrance to the Dewan-i-Khas one glimpses in the centre a square pool of water through the transparent columns of an intervening building, flanked to the right by the fantastic hovering terraces of the Panch Mahal and to the left by the curved roof of the state balcony overlooking the Dewan-i-Am. From the terraces of the Panch Mahal, the centre is occupied by the space of the Mahal-i-Khas framed by the flamboyant Dewan-i-Khas on the left and the rising structures of Akbar's private apartments on the right.

A panoramic field of vision, moving slowly through some 60° or 90° would seem to be nearer to the visual conception underlying this composition than a single piercing view that demands a central point of interest and undisturbing restful symmetry to either side of it.

It is possible that it just this panoramic view presented to a moving eye that gives the modern spectator such a feeling of intriguing relaxation at Fatehpur Sikri. But another key to its composition lies quite certainly in the fact that all dimensions, whether of the fashioning of spaces by the disposition of structures or of the spacing of columns, or the size and shape of openings and panels, must have been adjusted to a regulating scale of proportions based certainly upon the square, and probably upon the 'golden section'. In our Western 'academic' schools of architecture of the nineteenth century the 'golden section' was so mis-used that it became associated with the weakest forms of stylistic architectural mannerisms, but it is significant today that the greatest architect of our time and one of the leaders in the revolt against the dead hand of the academism of the 'beaux arts' schools, Le Corbusier, has recently re-developed a system of measurement of proportions based upon the 'golden section' under the name of the 'Modulor'.

It is now nearly half a century since Western artists and scientists started to break away from the tyranny of the static viewpoint—the conception of a static object and a static universe—to rediscover the importance of vision in motion. This close relationship of the discoveries of artists and scientists is not fortuitous: they are fundamentally one and the same. In Japan, it was not until near the end of the nineteenth century (after the penetration of Western thought) that there was any word in their language for 'Art', meaning 'fine art'. Until then 'Art' had just been 'the way of doing' things; whether solving a problem, building a house or preparing tea. There was 'the way', which was difficult and demanded imaginative intelligence and concentration, and there were poor substitutes of 'the way'. The 'artist' as an outcaste of normal society—a mere 'bohemian' or gypsy—is quite a recent Western invention.

Evidences of the fact that our Western vision is changing exist all around us, but most of them are left outside the realm of conscious rationalisation, because we have not yet learnt to organize them intellectually.

The moving eye is closely with us in the movies and on television. We see the scene from a certain viewpoint, then go nearer—not gradually but in one swoop—and then look at it again from a totally different angle. We accept this, because this is the way our eye really works: we can, at will, change its focus and alter its position. But we do not connote this at once with the changed appearance of contemporary painting, in which the significant features of these different viewpoints are often presented to us superimposed upon a single sheet: not in a time sequence but in juxtaposed fragments as, in fact, they are recorded by our mental vision. We have learnt to 'read' the rapid sequence of viewpoints at the movies, which baffle people who have not had long training in the art of 'movie-seeing', but most of us have not given ourselves much practice in learning to read contemporary paintings.

Today we stand before Versailles and are outwardly—and rightly—impressed (but inwardly we find it rather boring). We move along Main Street at night and outwardly—and rightly—confess it is a chaotic mess (but inwardly we find it rather exhilarating). Here is our contemporary urban planning problem. How to find the key to an intellectual system that will help us to organise buildings, colour, and movement in space, without relying entirely upon either introspective 'intuition' ('I *feel* it to be right that way') or upon the obsolete and static single viewpoint based on the limited optical science of the Renaissance.

J. Tyrwhitt

Explorations 3 described in detail an experiment conducted by a Communications Seminar at the University of Toronto in February, 1954, to test learning via various media. The experiment has since been summarized in a number of journals, but unfortunately this interest has not always been accompanied by understanding. We will not summarize the experiment here; the reader is referred to the original reports, in full.

In October, 1954, the original test was re-administered to the 74 students available of the 108 who took part in the first experiment. They were unaware beforehand that a re-examination was intended.

The multiple choice questionnaire used had 19 items, each with four alternative answers. It could be expected that a group knowing nothing of the subject would get 25% of the answers correct by guessing. Our subjects, however, were university Arts students who had taken courses in the social sciences and who could be assumed to do better than chance, even if they had neither seen nor heard the lecture. To check this, a control group was used: the questionnaire was given to 15 Second Year Honour psychology students, selected because, though their general training in social sciences was similar to the experimental group's, the lecture was unknown to them and they had received no instruction from the lecturer.

During the eight-month interval some students had heard the lecture a second time when its kinescope was shown on television to the general public and some may have discussed it with friends. It is assumed here, however, that such reinforcement was random. To determine whether or not the 74 students re-examined were representative of the original 108, we compared the performance means of the two groups (Figure 1). Although in each case the re-test means were slightly lower, these differences were fairly uniform, not great, and therefore, not fatal.

It was anticipated that on the average the re-examination marks would be significantly lower than the ones obtained on the first test. It was further assumed that if the media did not continue to influence the retention of learning over time, there would be no 'real' differences on the re-test among the four groups who received this lecture through different media. If significant differences were found on re-examination among the groups, this could be fairly attributed to differential effects of the media through which the information was originally obtained.
The results of the two tests for the 74 students are shown in Figure 1, broken down into the four groups, each of which was exposed to one medium. For comparison, the mean percentages of the original four groups are also given.

Two questions were considered: Were the media differences demonstrated by the first experiment still demonstrable after eight months? Did the media have a differential effect on forgetting during this period?

An affirmative answer to the first question was obtained by an analysis of variance of the means of the groups on the second test. It was found that there were still significant differences (*i.e.*, could have occurred by chance only once in 100 times) between them. Unfortunately, it was not possible to analyse these results in more detail since there were unequal losses in subjects in the four groups, so that further comparisons were not statistically justifiable. The answer to the first question is, however, clear: after eight months significant differences exist between the groups exposed to the different media. The results showed there had been one change in the order of ranking the four media: the studio group moved from last to second place. The results from this group were regarded with doubt in the original experiment and were not included in the conclusions; no interpretation is now made of this change in rank.

In order to answer the second question, it is necessary to compare the

116

	RETEST GROUP			ORIGINAL GROUP	
	First Test %	Second Test %		Test % First	
Television	75.4	61.5	14	77.2	27
Radio	65.5	52.6	21	69.2	27
Studio	62.9	56.0	21	64.9	27
Reading	63.9	47.5	18	65.1	27
			74		108

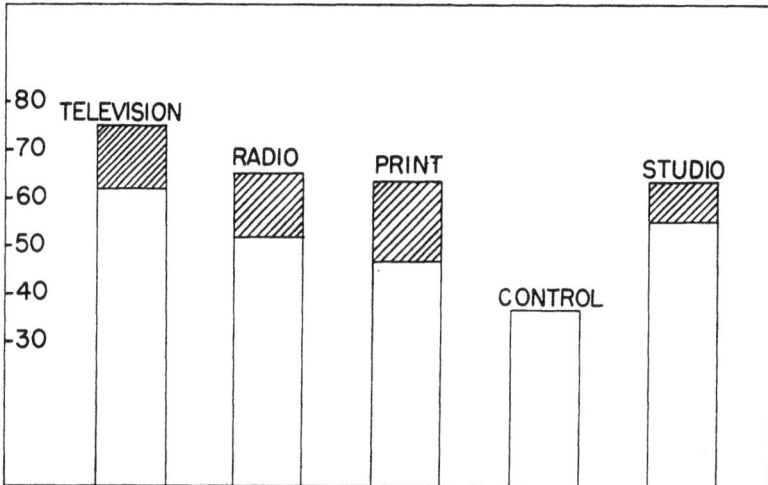

differences between the first and second tests for each group. The losses here when tested by analysis of variance could not be considered to differ significantly from each other. This implies that the amount retained after a period of time is proportional to the amount originally learned. In other words, the rate of forgetting information is independent of the medium by means of which it was acquired. This was graphically demonstrated, in that the original ranking of media in order of effectiveness—television, radio, print—held after eight months.

Since it was found that for every group the mean percentage for the second test was significantly lower than for the first test, a third question was asked. If, after eight months, the students have in general lower scores, how much better than intelligent guessing are their second test results? This is answered in Figure 1 in a comparison of their results with those of the control group of psychology students. Their scores are better than random guessing, but significantly lower than the lowest of the four media groups.

1:

In this particular experiment media made a difference in learning, not only in immediate recall, but after eight months. The original order of effectiveness—television, radio, print—held after this interval. In this experiment, different media influenced retention by influencing the amount of original learning.

The qualifications, given in *Explorations 3*, about misinterpretations of the original findings, apply to these later findings as well.

John Paul and John C. Ogilvie

Is the 'eye' the 'I'? Lee has shown how, in recent centuries, the self
has been divided in English into I, me, mine, that is, into consciousness
or mind, body, and possessions, with the I in control, e.g., I lift my foot,
and the passions below the I or mind, e.g., I fall in love or into a rage,
I delve into my subconscious. In many preliterate societies the centre of
the self, that which is eternal, is the name or word, the breath of life. If
the eye is the I, is this because ours is not an oral, but a written, visual
tradition? Etymologically, there's no support for the eye being the I,
but—

目

Though the poet ought to write as if his work were intended to be read
aloud, in practice the reading aloud of a poem distracts attention from its
subtler properties by emphasizing the more obvious ones. The outward
ear is easily deceived. A beautiful voice can make magic even with bad

or fraudulent poetry which the eye, as the most sophisticated organ of sense, would reject at once; for the eye is in close communication with the undeceivable inward ear.

Robert Graves

印 1

I am the Man in the Cloak. In other words, I am by no manner of means the Man *of* the Cloak or the Man *under* the Cloak. The Germans call me *'Der Mensch mit dem Mantel'*, the Man with the Cloak. This is a deplorable error in the nomenclature of that otherwise intelligent people: because my cloak is not part and parcel of myself. The cloak is outside and the man inside, but each is a distinct entity. I admit you may say, 'The Man with the Greasy Countenance', thus also Slawken-Bergius (*vide* 'Tristram Shandy') calls his hero 'The Stranger with the Nose', for, however long, the nose was an integral part of the individual. With me the case is a horse of a different colour. I do not put my cloak on and off, I grant, but I can do so when I please: and therefore it is obvious to the meanest capacity that I am the Man *in* the Cloak and no mistake. [This objection to the German idiom could have been strengthened by an opposite objection to the French *'l'homme à la redingote'*, where greater emphasis is laid on the cloak than on the man. The author, as he says, is not 'the Man *of* the Cloak'; yet, *'l'homme dans la redingote'* is no more French than *'Der Mensch in dem Mantel'* is German.]

James Clarence Mangan

男

A standard language is, under modern conditions, a written rather than a spoken language. The printed word becomes more and more the reality, the spoken word an echo or faint copy of it. This inversion of the normal relation between speech and writing, this predominance of the eye over the ear, of the written symbol over its audible equivalent, tends to deprive the language of that vigour and reality which comes, and can only come, from its intimate association with the acts and passion of men, as they vividly describe and express them in their speech. Freed from the necessity of using terms which can be easily spoken and understood, and more concerned with abstract thought than feeling, the written language, when it finds new terms are necessary, supplies its needs by borrowing learned words, or by making long compounds out of Greek or Latin elements. It is by means of these mechanical or dead words that it tries to make up for its lack of original power; and their abundant use, and the mechanical ease by which they can be formed, tend in their turn to cripple still further what creative powers the language may still possess.

Logan Pearsall Smith

說

When 'primitives' are said to be incapable of distinguishing the word from the *thing*, or to confuse an object with its name, I suspect that what we have is rather the recognition of this participation of the symbol in the *thing*. When we reflect on our own use of words, we find that with us also, words do more than designate; they have more or less meaning, according to the situations in our personal lives in which they have participated. For example, when I teach, I can use terms for the function of evacuation and for sexual activity freely, so long as I confine myself to Latin words. Otherwise there is discomfort and emotional tension. This does not mean that the Latin terms do not carry the situation in which they have participated. They do; but what they convey is the passage in the textbook, or the paragraph in the dictionary; and these are eminently appropriate for the classroom. When I use the word, 'micturation', it carries with it, perhaps, a number of defining words, but not the concrete act. Anglo-Saxon terms for sexual activity would heighten the emotional atmosphere and be very disturbing in the classroom. But not so the Latin terms; they may have participated in love-making in the experience of the Romans, but nobody makes love in Latin nowadays.

This is also true of the words for death or dying. Those of us who have experienced death tend to avoid the symbolizing word in speaking of these situations, because the word conveys the unbearable situation. The need for a term is filled then by a number of substitute terms, such as 'passed away', or by differently phrased sentences which avoid the charged word. Yet none of us feels the urge to do this when speaking of people we have not loved. Julius Caesar died; he did not pass away.

Dorothy Lee

Whereas we are trained to think scientifically, many primitive peoples are trained to think poetically. Because we are literate, we tend to credit words with exact meanings—dictionary meanings. Our whole education is designed to make language a more precise scientific instrument. The ordinary speech of an educated man is expected to conform to the canons of prose rather than of poetry; ambiguity of statement is deplored. But in primitive society the reverse may be the case; a faculty for making and understanding ambiguous statements may even be cultivated. In many parts of Asia, for example, we find variants of a courtship game the essence of which is that the young man first recites a verse of poetry which is formally innocent but amorous by innuendo. The girl must then reply with another poem which matches the first not only in its overt theme, but also in its erotic covert meaning. People who use language in this way become highly adept at understanding symbolic statements. This applies not only to words but also to the motifs and arrangements of material designs.

Edmund Leach

Perhaps the greatest reason why inventions seem to decline, is that they change out of their definition. If an invention were defined with highest precision, it could never be improved at all; for the least change would move the thing out of the definition. The definition makes the invention, which probably has no definition aside from language and other social habits.

S. C. Gilfillan

先

All that goes to constitute a gentleman—the carriage, gait, address, gestures, voice; the ease, the self-possession, the courtesy, the power of conversing, the success in not offending; the lofty principle, the delicacy of thought, the happiness of expression, the taste and propriety, the generosity and forbearance, the candour and consideration, the openness of hand—these qualities, some of them come by nature, some of them may be found in any rank, some of them are a direct precept of Christianity; but the full assemblage of them, bound up in the unity of an individual character, do we expect they can be learned from books?

The great instrument, or rather organ, of religious teaching has ever been that which nature prescribes in all education, the personal presence of the teacher, or, in theological language, Oral Tradition. It is the living voice, the breathing form, the expressive countenance, which preaches, which catechises.

Cardinal Newman

心

In de-coding, a message may be corrected, *e.g.*, the unconscious correction of mispronunciations and the addition of omitted or drowned out words. De-coding may also distort to the point of producing a new one. But how far can it go in actually creating messages out of whole cloth? In divination—Chinese sticks, I Ching, African bones, jacks, crystals, tea leaves, palms, scapulas—the practitioner creates a meaningless, non-symbolic field, like Rorschach, from (into, we would say) which he then reads his message. Just as in the allophone, that projective test of meaningless sounds which the subject is asked to interpret, so at the clap of thunder, an old Indian woman asks, 'What did he say?' and her husband replies, 'He said . . . .'

天

'No – I assure you – now er – er – that – er – it was the most shocking accident possible – er – poor Chester was riding in the Park – er – you know that grey – er [substantive dropped, hand a little flourished instead] – of his – splendid creature! – er – well sir, and by Jove – er – the – er – [no substantive, flourish again] – took fright, and – e – er –' here the gentleman throws up his chin and eyes, sinks back exhausted into his chair, and after a pause adds, 'Well, they took him into – the shop – there – you know – with the mahogany sashes – just by the Park – er – and the – er – man there – set his – what d'ye call it – er – collar-bone; *but* he was – er ter-ri-bly – terribly' – a full stop. The gentleman shakes his head – and the sentence is suspended to eternity. Another gentleman takes up the wondrous tale thus logically: 'Ah! shocking, shocking! – *but* poor Chester was a very agreeable – er' – full stop!

'O! devilish gentlemanlike fellow! — quite shocking! — quite — did you go into the – er – today?'

'No, indeed; the day was so *un* – may I take some wine with you?'

Edward Lytton Bulver

There is hardly a polite sentence in the following dialogues which doth not absolutely require some peculiar graceful motion in the eyes, or nose, or mouth, or forehead, or chin, or suitable toss of the head, with certain offices assigned to each hand; and in ladies, the whole exercise of the fan, fitted to the energy of every word they deliver; by no means omitting the various turns and cadence of the body; the several kinds and gradations of laughter, which the ladies must daily practice by the looking-glass, and consult upon with their waiting-maids.

Jonathan Swift

If I had to choose between a so-called university, which dispensed with residence and tutorial superintendence, and gave its degrees to any person who passed an examination in a wide range of subjects, and a university which had no professors or examinations at all, but merely brought a number of young men together for three or four years, and then sent them away as the University of Oxford is said to have done some sixty years since, if I were asked which of these two methods was the better discipline of the intellect, — mind, I do not say which is morally the better, for it is plain that compulsory study must be a good and idleness an intolerable mischief, — but if I must determine which of the two courses was the more successful in training, molding, enlarging the mind, which sent out men the more fitted for their secular duties, which produced better public men, men of the world, men whose names would descend to posterity, I have no hesitation in giving the preference to that university which did nothing, over that which exacted of its members an acquaintance with every science under the sun.

Cardinal Newman

叫

Plato's *Republic* presents a utopia with very little visual appeal. It is a utopia for the ear by comparison with the Medieval and Renaissance utopias. More recently it appears that there is a divergence between utopian and messianic dreaming of the future. The utopians resort to spatial projection of their ideas. The messianic Marxists, postulating human prefectibility in time, avoid such spatial imagery. An Orwell has only to translate their time dream into space terms to make the messianic appear the horrific.

夕

It is significant that in our everyday activities we equate 'space' with 'room'. Our spatial notions probably come from our childhood experience of exploring rectangular rooms with rigid boundaries which are filled with objects arranged in precise order according to the commands of a parent. Later the idea of measurement was added. In one African community I know well, people do not think of space in these ways. For them space is equated with emptiness, in one sense, with direction in another. I think this has a close connection with their mode of living in round huts which are almost devoid of furniture. As a matter of fact, they can hardly be said to live *in* their huts. Their daytime life is public and shared with the whole world, for it is carried on in the open court- yards of the homestead or under the shade tree in front. They do not experience space as made up of regular closed-in units or shapes. Whenever boys and girls came to visit me I used to give them crayons to amuse themselves with. They would scribble and draw energetically until they had covered the whole sheet of paper. But what was striking was the surprise they showed when they came to the edge of the paper, as if they quite expected the blank space to stretch infinitely in all directions.

Meyer Fortes

山

Recalling in tranquillity the slow possession of Britain by its people, I cannot resist the conclusion that the relationship reached its greatest intimacy, its most sensitive pitch, about two hundred years ago. By the middle of the eighteenth century men had triumphed, the land was theirs, but had not yet been subjected and outraged. Wildness had been pushed back to the mountains, where now for the first time it could safely be admired. Communications were good enough to bind the country in a unity lacking since it was a Roman province, but were not as yet so easy as to have destroyed locality and the natural freedom of the individual that remoteness freely gives. Rich men and poor men knew how to use the stuff of their countryside to raise comely buildings and to group them with instinctive grace. Town and country having grown up together to serve one another's needs now enjoyed a moment of balance.

Jacquetta Hawkes

水

The normal European idea of a house is a structure containing a number of box-like enclosures or rooms, each bounded by four walls, a floor and a ceiling: these being conceived as flat, opaque surfaces pierced by windows and doors that can be opened and closed at will. Even when a surface is made completely transparent, it still remains a glass *wall*. In its simplest form, the Western dwelling is a single room, within which a man can exist in reasonable comfort the year around by judicious adjustment of the openings, and perhaps the addition of a heating unit.

This concept was foreign to south-east Asia before the advent of Western ideas. In the difficult climate of northern and central India, for instance, the minimum area for year-round existence is not a single 'room' in the Western sense, but three different types of private space. The first is an open court, or a roof-top, which serves as a general living space through-out the bright, dry days of winter, and as a sleeping area during the oppressively hot summer months when it is impossible to be inside, as every wall emits all the heat it has absorbed during the day—like the walls of a baking oven. The second space is roofed but unwalled, though it may take the compromise form of a verandah. Here one lives and sleeps throughout the steamy heat of the rainy season, welcoming every slight and shifting breeze. The third space—the smallest and least fre-quently used—is a completely enclosed, double walled and double roofed box, into which no sunlight can ever penetrate: ventilated by tiny slits just under the roof. Here, at mid-day, one can take cool refuge from the blazing summer heat, and here one can retire for warmth during the chilly nights of winter. This is the only one of the three spaces that corresponds to the Western 'room', and for the most part of the year it is merely used as a storage space—a cupboard.

All Indian furniture is light and portable: a light wooden frame with a woven cover, some cushions, and perhaps a low table, are all the furniture necessary for comfort, even luxury. All cooking is done in the open air on a small charcoal stove that is almost equally portable. Those who live in palaces, and who have not adopted Western ways, can and do change the part of their residence in which they wish to live at a moment's notice and with no fuss, according to the mood of the weather.

This marvelously flexible, pleasant, and economic conception of human living space no longer exists in contemporary houses built in India for the well-to-do, with very few exceptions. It can, however, be found, in a rudimentary form, in almost all the village houses—built of mud—and in the old Moghul mansions and palaces.

Nowadays, when we of the West are just beginning again to find the pleasure of living in an 'open plan'—due to our having conquered climatic changes with air conditioning and central heating—the modern Indian only considers himself up-to-date if he lives in a thoroughly enclosed 'European' box of rooms. We, in our development of the cult of the barbecue, the sun terrace, and the sleeping deck, are but re-discovering the high civilisation of the East of some centuries ago.

東

1

In the latter half of the 19th century, Dr. Edwin Abbott published a science fiction work called *Flatland*. In it he pictures intelligent beings whose whole experience is confined to a plane, or other space of two dimensions, who have no faculties by which they can become conscious of anything outside that space and no means of moving off the surface on which they live. He then asks the reader, who has the consciousness of the third dimension, to imagine a sphere descending upon the plane of Flatland and passing through it. How will the inhabitants regard this phenomenon? They will not see the approaching sphere and will have no conception of its solidarity. They will only be conscious of the circle in which it cuts their plane. This circle, at first a point, will gradually increase in diameter, bring the inhabitants of Flatland outwards from its circumference, and this will go on until half the sphere has passed through the plane, when the circle will gradually contract to a point and then vanish, leaving the Flatlanders in undisturbed possession of their country. Their experience will be that of a circular obstacle gradually expanding and growing, and then contracting, and they will attribute to *growth in time* what the external observer in three dimensions assigns to motion in the third dimension. Transfer this analogy to a movement of the fourth dimension through three-dimensional space. Assume the past and future of the universe to be all depicted in four-dimensional space and visible to any being who has consciousness of the fourth dimension. If there is motion of our three-dimensional space relative to the fourth dimension, all the changes we experience and assign to the flow of time will be due simply to this movement, the whole of the future as well as the past always existing in the fourth dimension. At the end of the novel the hero is taken by a Stranger to Spaceland and there, after great difficulty, is able to conceive of a sphere, but when he asks the Stranger if there is a land of Four Dimensions, or Five or Six, he is told, 'There is no such land.'

月

Fredric Wertham writes: 'In our studies we found marked differences between the media in their effect on children. The passivity is greatest in reading comic books, perhaps a little less with television, if only because other people are present in the audience. In both, the entertainment flows over the child. Passivity is least in going to movies, where others are always present.'

Wertham has not considered the implications of this statement for the printed book. The transportable printed book brought into existence the solitary, silent reader. The book established that divorce between 'literature and life' which was unknown to ages in which the transmission of wisdom was oral. According to Wertham, 'Reading disorders are much more frequent in some countries than in others—in the United States and England, for example, rather than Germany. In a study of 51,000 children in the schools of Munich, contrary to expectation, only ten were found (ages ten to fourteen) with serious reading disorders.' In other words, Dr. Wertham assumes reading as the norm of mental health without ever having considered the psychological and cultural effects of this extremely artificial activity.

書

Violence is the constant theme of comic books and animated cartoons. Not only violence to others, but violence of achievement and performance of extravagant acts by heros, heroines, and animals. May not such violence merely be the unwitting projection into the visual world of the fantastic power of mechanism and technology? May not the taste for violence in thriller fiction, in the daily press, magazines, and movies be the projection of the effect of *living with* machines? May not the mere vibration of the internal combustion engine and of electric machines impart a non-human tempo and rhythm to ordinary existence which in turn evoke the extravagant in fiction, news and art?

Effective censorship can only be known to the censors; as soon as it becomes involved in controversy, its effectiveness declines. In its most responsible phases, censorship is applied to help maintain the minimum agreement required to hold a society together. In its less responsible phases, it is the result of self-interested pressure groups. In both, it is concerned with minimizing awareness of specific subjects, that is, blocking communication. Consequently the censor argues that when censorship must be applied, the less said or known about it the better. The most efficient censorship is secret; the best censors don't talk.

In an age of specialization, method is more important than information.

Walter Gropius

American newspapers attacked patent medicines and advocated pure food and drug laws as a device for weakening the position of lower grade newspapers and periodicals dependent on this type of advertising. When radio came to Canada, the newspapers, viewing it as a competitor for advertising, strongly supported the establishment of the nationalized Canadian Broadcasting Corporation. But when radio proved a boon, not a threat to newspaper advertising, and when, moreover, publishers bought into private radio, the newspapers turned against CBC with a vengeance.

In the course of regulating radio, a principle startlingly new in its implications to traditional American concepts has been introduced—an extension, if you like, of the principle of free speech. This is the doctrine that when certain controversial subjects are discussed over the air, both sides must be given an equal amount of time. To be sure, in some cases it is impossible to exercise this right, since, if time has been paid for by one side, the other side may not have money enough to meet the high cost of radio time. But in general the very notion presents a definite enlargement of the concept of free expression. It says, in effect, that we are no longer merely concerned, as we were in the eighteenth century, lest some authority prevent a man from saying what he wants to. It says, in addition, that those who control limited channels for reaching the public have an obligation to present both sides of controversial issues.

In one city I know, the only morning and the only evening papers and one of the radio and television stations are owned by the same man, who happens to apply the highest standards of responsibility. He has no competition in the newspaper field, but has in radio and television. The latter are strictly regulated and his license to operate, his very right to exist, must be periodically reviewed and renewed by the Federal Communications Commission. In the field in which he is a monopolist—and it may be interesting to note that at one time there were four other newspaper owners in his city—no one would dare interfere with his rights of free enterprise or free press. This situation is not unique. In most of our cities there is now less competition in newspapers than in broadcasting.

Harold K. Guinzburg

131

The fox knows many things
But the hedgehog knows one big thing
                                    Archilochus

BLAST

The Hedgehog
  massive
  obstinate
  dedicated
  determined to reduce the immense variety of human experience to:

              a single all-embracing system
                          or
              a single all-explanatory principle

  Blast Plato, Dante, Hegel, Proust, Lenin, Hitler, Eliot, Harpo Marx

  Blast all hedgehogs

BLESS

The fox
  quick
  curious
  sceptical
  revelling in:

                  the inexhaustible diversity
                             and
                  pluralism of life and faith

  Bless Shakespeare, Goethe, Joyce, James, Russell, Groucho Marx

  Bless all foxes

要

There are two ways in which experience is integrated or learned; as in the case of sex, these do not exist in their pure state, *i.e.*, each has characteristics of the other in varying degrees and there are inter-grades. These two exist in complementary relationship to each other and are both necessary; also, as in the case of the sexes, different cultures may enhance or value or emphasize one more than the other. Within each there will be a hierarchy; just as some men are more masculine than others and some women more feminine, there is also a hierarchy within the two types of integration.

In order to avoid invidious differentiations, we have termed these two *point* and *line* integration. Both can be either high or low order in their own class, or they can fall between extremes. They are characterized as follows:

The line integrator works within a given system or systems. His function is to make systems go, and his intellectual eyes are turned inward, as it were, towards improving and working within, or manipulating his own frame of reference. When he is a high order line integrator, he learns very rapidly and with great ease, so long as what is given him is integrated into some type of system. Memory work is not arduous to him. By and large he ignores contradictions between the internal logic of his own systems and events which are outside his systems. It must not be assumed that line integrators are not scientists; one can say that some of the best scientific work is done by persons of this type. This is because, given a system, they then go to work and build the solid foundation which gives the system substance.

This type has an easy time in school if he is 'bright', because he does not tend to question the system but accepts it as given him. He is, however, at times disturbed by and tends to distrust the point integrator who raises questions about points that are outside the line integrator's systems. Some figures of speech associated with this type are as follows: 'Now I get (or don't get) the picture', 'Let me sketch you in', 'I can't quite take this in'.

The point integrator has to make each point his very own, and consequently may learn more slowly than a line integrator. He is likely to

133

question his teachers and professors about the 'principles' involved in a given scheme. He is deeply disturbed by contradictions, either within a given frame of reference or between that frame of reference and what is outside. There are times when he has difficulty with the line integrators who do not get his points. His function in regard to society is to create new systems as conditions change; he is, however, restless in a static situation and tends to suffer if he isn't permitted to integrate his points. Having discovered the points, however, he is likely to lose interest and move on, leaving line integrators to fill in the picture, so that in the realm of science he is often accused of being 'unscientific' or lacking proof for his points. Einstein would be an example of a point integrator of the highest order, Napier of a line integrator. No one can deny the contribution of either.

Point integrators tend to use figures of speech somewhat as follows: 'Let's get down to cases', 'Now I get (or don't get) the point', 'Somehow I can't seem to grasp what he is talking about', 'I need something tangible to get hold of', 'That brings it into focus', 'Can't you pin-point it a little more?' Point integrators seem to get very excited or centre their emotions on ideas, whereas the line integrator has visceral reactions when his systems (which are seen as involving moral principles) are violated.

E. T. Hall, Jr., and G. L. Trager

The talking musical instruments of Negro Africa fill a range of roles in African culture similar to those of our pipe-organs, orchestras, jazz bands, mass propaganda media, and telegraph systems. They supply the rhythms and music for the recreational 'Club' dances; they play for the most formal funerals and public festivals; they accompany the dances of the ancestral masks and the society masks; they supply a running commentary on inquest and court proceedings; they propagandize for war and for peace; they praise famous men; they provide a ready means of communication over long distances. At a big public ceremony, the great drums may review much of the group's history and intone the most sacred truths known to the people.

In this discussion I shall mainly use illustrations and general statements drawn from my own fieldwork with the Idoma-speaking peoples of Benue Province, Nigeria. For more general treatments of the subject, the reader may turn to Rattray's various works on Ashanti or to Carrington's more recent work.

Talking musical instruments in Africa usually do not transmit a code or cipher. Rather they send that definite pattern of sounds taken from the whole speech utterance which can be imitated by the instrument. The tonal quality of most African languages is of great assistance in this regard, and the West African languages in particular are very tonal indeed. The various instruments used can usually imitate and transmit the tones, the stresses (where these are phonemic), and the number of syllables in the utterance. It can be seen that this leaves considerable room for ambiguity in short, non-standard utterances, unless the social context sufficiently limits the possible interpretations.

Pike's *Tone Languages* distinguishes two general types of tone system: 'gliding-pitch contour systems' and 'level-pitch register systems'. He also recognizes the existence of mixed systems. In a contour system, like Mandarin Chinese, the glides and their direction of movement are basic to the system. In principle the various words in a set differentiated by tone alone can be distinguished from each other when uttered in isolation. Thus we have ma⁻ (high-level), ma⁄ (high-rising), maᵛ (falling-and-rising), and maˋ (falling). It is hard to see how a drum or other instrument could 'talk' in such a system unless, like the trombone or like the under-arm strong-controlled drum of West Africa, it is capable of doing *glissandi*. Most African languages have level-pitch register tone systems. In these the pitch of a syllable, 'within the limits of perception', does not rise or fall during its pronunciation. Languages with two, three, and four tonemic levels are known from West Africa. Idoma has three phonemic, or 'tonemic', tone levels, although five can be distinguished phonetically.

It goes without saying that the actual pitch values of the registers is relative. A high tone is a tone which is level with or above any other tone which may occur in its immediate vicinity. The other tones may be defined in similar terms. Monosyllabic words distinguished only by tone in such a system cannot in principle be identified when uttered in isolation. Thus, to take three common verbs in Idoma, we have má, to see, mǎ, to quit, and mà, to give birth to (high, mid, and low tones, respectively). If I say simply 'ma', the listener has no way of knowing which was intended. The moment there are two or three syllables of context, however, the listener has a measure of relative pitch and will understand. Isolated two-syllable words alike but for tone are readily distinguishable from each other by the native speaker, even when they occur in so extended a set as: ìgwù, guinea-corn; ìgwǔ, a hump, convexity; ìgwú, a call, shout; ígwú, history; and ígwù, a group, a class. (For the rest of this paper, the low tone will usually be unmarked, since in Idoma it is the most frequent). Phonetically speaking, gliding tones do occur in register systems. They are very frequent in Idoma. In a pure register system, they can all be analysed in terms of their end points: 'They may be considered as two or more tonemes juxtaposed'.

Features of stress and juncture may also accompany these 'glides' and help set them off. In Idoma it is convenient to consider such vowels as 'linked', according to the following rules, first stated by Major R. C. Abraham:
1. All non-linked syllables in Idoma have equal stress and length. Every syllable has one and only one vowel or syllabic (m, n, ŋ, ŋm, l, r), usually characterized by a single breath pulse and by a slight diminution of breath between syllables (óócí, tomorrow; mùṁṁ? bore me? pɔ̌ɔ̌ɔ̌? peeled it?).
2. Vowels and nasal syllabics link when the same vowel or nasal succeeds itself on a different tone level, or when a nasal follows a vowel on a different tone level.
   a. A linked pair of vowels has less than twice the length of a single vowel.
   b. The first member of a linked pair is stressed more than the average covered in Rule 1. The second member is weakened below this level. The juncture between them is a quick glide without the diminution of breadth of rule 1a (mɔ̌ɔ̌, saw him; mɔ́ɔ, saw you; múm, saw me; aíŋm gbo, my children began; năa, that you (sing.) . . .)
   c. If the vowel is tripled on three tone levels, or if a vowel is followed by two nasals on different tone levels, a pivot linkage results. The middle member of the triplet is stressed and the first and third are weakened (năaá, that you (pl.); eyŋkpɔ̌, water; aáa, they (indirect discourse).
   d. If the vowel or nasal is doubled on either the first or second tone level of a pair, there is no linkage (ijeéékpó, one fly; máǎ? saw you (pl.)? múmm? saw me?).
3. The junctures between morphological words have not yet been shown to differ from the junctures between syllables.

Thus we have mǎa, the demonstrative 'this'; maá, 'gave birth to you' (pl.); ma ǎa, '[whom she] bore'; maá ǎa, '... [who] bore you' (pl.); mǎá tá, 'left you'; mǎáá ta, 'left your children'; máá, 'saw you'; mááá, 'saw your children'; mááá ǎǎ, '... [who] saw your children'; etc. The interrogative may be formed by doubling the mid or low tone final vowel or by doubling the final high tone vowel on mid without linkage. This gives us such interrogative forms as maa? mǎǎ? máǎǎ? maáǎǎ? mǎáǎǎ? mááǎ? etc. There is another emphatic final particle á which may occur with every one of the above constructions, both in the positive or in the ǎǎ ǎ? interrogative form. (It should be noted that the existing orthographies in use in Idoma and in Nigeria generally write everything on the above list as ma, or perhaps mǎ which must therefore do duty for at least thirty quite different utterances).

It may be seen that a flute, a xylophone, or a set of drums can easily reproduce the essential features of such a tonal system. One can also whistle all these forms. It must not be thought, however, that to understand their 'speech' it is sufficient to know the tones of the 'absolute' forms of the words: the forms as one might find them listed in a lexicon. The drums follow the spoken language, not the lexicon. The study of the morphonology, the systematic changes which the speech sounds undergo when they enter into syntactic and morphological context, has been the Mt. Everest of West African language studies up till the very present. The foreigner carefully learns the tones of a word, and then finds to his horror that the tones change radically and vowels drop out right and left the moment the words are used in a sentence. The complete utterance differs very much from a string of corresponding morphemes pronounced or written in their 'absolute' or lexical form. This fact also makes it hard for the native speakers to identify a word securely as it appears in context. Without such secure identifications, no solid dictionary can be built—a statement only too well supported by the absence, even after all these years of European contact, of useable dictionaries of such language as Yoruba and Ibo.

For example, in Idoma compound words, the most common form of morpheme juncture involves the exchange of vowel and tone. The last syllable of the first simple word loses its vowel, but confers its tone on the first syllable of the following word. Thus we have the word idɔ̌ma and the word ɔcέ, 'chief, king' (c/ = ch in church). The Chief of Idoma is ɔcídɔ̌ma. ɔcέ has lost its /ε/ and the /i-/ of idɔ̌ma has moved from low tone to high tone. If we say, 'I saw the Chief of Idoma', using the verb má, 'to see', and m̀, the first person pronoun, the full utterance, is m mɔ́cídɔ̌ma. The vowel of má is lost, and the /ɔ-/ of ɔcέ has moved from low to high. If the drum or the flute were to give out the tones of the separate morphemes m má ɔcέ iďma, its pattern would be \/ \/ / V \. The pattern of the actual transmission is \/ / V \, which corresponds to the normal utterance. Suspension of an expected elision gives an adverbial meaning. Thus, m mɔ́cέ idɔ̌ma means, 'I saw a chief in Idoma.'

In other circumstances (*e.g.*, before two low tones) morphemes are joined by linking. Thus Chief of Otukpó is ɔcóotukpó.

In the early stages of study of one of these languages, it is fiendishly hard to get reliable examples of this sort from the ordinary informant whom the linguist is apt to have. One will choose a person with as much education in English as possible, and yet considerations other than education must be taken into account. Mission and Government education in Nigeria as yet pay no attention to tone or to morphophonology; and this is the education which has shaped the informant's notion of his language, if he is literate. The minute the informant starts thinking about an utterance, he tries to analyse it for you into its constituent morphemes. He cannot do this consistently; but he nevertheless resists the normal spoken form, which he now tells you is 'colloquial'. If one presses the point, one gets oneself into the position of wishing to make a permanent record of colloquial speech, to the exclusion of the 'classical', 'literary' language. Thus a political strain may enter the interview situation. I am not exaggerating.

One must constantly seek ways of helping the informant give the morpheme junctures correctly and unself-consciously. The talking instruments are extremely useful for this, and above all the method of whistling which requires no apparatus. When one is making one's first notes on a new language, the informant often gets tired. When this happens the difference in pitch between the several tones of his utterances usually gets to be very slight; and he will slur over many other fine distinctions. Asking for too many repetitions only makes the situation worse, for he may start giving the tones wrongly. Asking him to whistle the word or phrase gives an entirely fresh clue to his tonal and syllabic intentions and adds variety to his task. It is not sufficient to rely on whistling alone, for whistling may introduce its own errors. But on hundreds of occasions the whistled form of a word or phrase drew my attention to some distinction which had escaped my ear completely in the spoken form. In fact it takes considerable practice for a European to hear in speech many things which are clear enough when whistled. Whistling is just as useful when one is deep in the language as when one is beginning, for then one will be working with much more sophisticated texts, full of tricky constructions and subtle nuances. The proverbs, too, are full of arbitrary sound changes, forms from other dialects, archaic forms and foreign words. It is precisely in these qualities that much of their 'flavour' and their heuristic value lies. It requires all the technique at one's command to record and interpret them correctly.

I did not find that whistling was as highly developed as an art or as a means of communication in Idoma as has been reported from other parts of Africa. It is used mainly by children, and as a rule they are much better at whistling than older people. On the other hand, I had no difficulty in introducing it as a tool into the interview situation from the very beginning in languages and places as diverse as Yoruba, Ibo, Igala, Bassa Komo, Uffá, Obanliko, Betě, Etulŏ, Berom, Égĕdĕ and Akwéya. I would start the inter-view by asking for some such word as 'goat'. When I got it, I would ask, 'Will you whistle it?' In every one of the above cases, the informant did so readily.

The famous talking drums of Africa may be divided into two principal types, the membrane drums and the slit-log gongs. Membrane drums may be used as in the Gold Coast, where two drums of different size are used to talk. In Idoma, this is little seen except in certain ceremonies. A double-ended drum with an hour-glass shape and many thongs connecting and tightening the two heads is very common in West Africa. It is seen in Hausa, Yoruba, Tiv and Igala country in Nigeria and in the Niger Bend region of the French Sudan. It is held under the left arm, which exerts varying pressure on the strings. This changes the tension on the drum heads and affects their pitch. This is a most flexible drum which, as has been mentioned above, can do glissandi. It is not popular in Idoma, where an open-ended drum, about a foot in diameter and two feet long is preferred. The drummer sits on this and plays it with his bare hands. He keeps one heel against the drumhead and with it varies the tension. By this means and by hitting the drum in the centre and on the edge—and even on the rim—he can get several tones. The chief drummer at a large dance will often use this drum, and with it he can achieve a control over the other drums and over the line of dancers that an orchestra conductor might envy. He can start the line dancing, change the dance several times without stopping it, call particular people out by name to solo, correct their dance, and send them back into line with comment on the performance. And all the while there may be from three to a dozen other drums playing.

The well-known slit-log gongs of Africa have been often described, and I have little to add to what Carrington has said in *Explorations 1*. The two lips of the gong are of different thicknesses and give notes of differing pitch when struck. Such a gong has no trouble handling a language with two phonemic tone levels. A pair of such gongs of different sizes can 'speak' a three-tone or a four-tone language with great clarity. I have heard such a pair used in this way in the royal compound of the Chief of Agala, to 'speak' the Agala dialect of Idoma. In practice, however, a single gong is usually used in Idoma and other Nigerian regions, although the languages have three, and in some cases (Egede, Igala) four phonemic tone levels. This poses a problem which I cannot entirely resolve. Unfortunately I have no tape recordings of log gongs 'speaking' Idoma. It is said that mid tones may be prouced on a single gong by striking both lips simultaneously. I made a considerable effort to confirm this, but was unable to do so. The question cannot be studied simply at one's convenience in the field. The large gongs are used to signal important events, such as the death of a senior elder or the outbreak of war. They are not played frivolously, for this would disturb many people. One must watch for an opportunity to practice or enquire about the technique of playing one when the drummer is resting at some big event when the gong is being used, unless one is willing to commit a serious breach of African etiquette. Even the small log gongs can only be played in a town or village with the specific permission of the elders. They may be played for practice or amusement on the farm, however. The drummers, however friendly they may be, are not eager to discuss their methods. The best drummer in my district was a particular friend of mine, but never seemed to find the right occasion to show me how he plays. One day in desperation I borrowed a small gong and went out and found him on his farm, where he had no excuse. He gave me a very good demonstration of rapid drumming in general and even agreed that one could strike both lips to produce a mid tone. But when I asked him to do it, he said that the gong I had was old and that the lips had been worn till they were too far apart. He would show me on a newer gong some time. A month later at a big dance, where he was using a very good large gong, I managed to corner him again. He did ɔcóotukpó and aóogwucé very nicely; but when I asked him to do aɔɔdaǐ (a well-known lineage name), he said, 'That is very hard', and either could not or would not do it.

If we assume that the gong cannot in any way produce three distinct tones (and some gongs give different notes from various points on the same lip), then it is obvious that the mid tone (the least frequent in Idoma) must in some way be assimilated either to the low or to the high. There may, of course, be some tendency to prefer transmissions which contain only two of the three possible tone levels. Three of the six drum statements given below are of this nature. More important, to my mind, is another feature of tone languages: The important thing is not the pitch—not even the relative pitch—of the syllables, but rather what we may call the fulcra of movement. The crucial matter is to know when to remain on an even pitch level, when to go up or down, and the direction of movement. For example, I collected the following title in the field from a gong transmission: otɔcí lǎnyǐkwǔŋ! 'He who climbs trees and fears ('saves') not death!' [o-, agent/tǔ, to climb/ ɔcí, tree; /ǎ, to save/ǎnyǐ, economy/ikwǎ, death/,ŋ not]. If we consider (knowing also how this sounds in speech) how this might be sent using only two notes, it is evident that whatever happens to the first two syllables, the drum must rise to the -cí syllable. The next three syllables must be lower than -cí and the final -ǔʏ are a linked pair, in which the -ǔ- is stressed and the -ʏ is weakened. This last can only happen if -ʏ is on a different, and in this case higher, tone level than -ǔ-. It thus seems most probable that in this transmission all the mid tones are assimilated to the low, since this will satisfy the requirements mentioned. It seems to me that the transmission here must have been \\ / \\\/, (the last two notes underlined to show linkage).

This was collected from the large gong, known as agidigbé, which apart from announcements of important deaths and war is used only to accompany the dances of the warlike secret men's societies. Several other typical messages of this latter type from this gong are:

Otkɔ́pa kwɔ́ɔgɔ! 'The spear-thrower catches the kite-hawk' (title of the ring-leader of the dancers).
Okwɔga ɔlá! 'He who thrusts strangers into the fire!'
Otɔ́cí ligbóligbó! 'He who climbs far!'
Okwŭ cɛga nó ce gĕdĕgĕdĕ! 'A corpse lies in a place: it lies in plain sight ('clear!')'
Onmóolikpó tumɛtumɛ! 'The killer of short-legged things!' (i.e., goats, which the society is famous for stealing on the nights when it meets to dance).

Several varieties of horns are used by the Idoma, all being of the common African transverse variety, blown from the side. The pointed end of the horn has a small hole drilled in it which is opened or closed by the thumb. The palm of the hand controls the large opening. The largest horns consist of long, narrow gourds fitted together to make a long instrument with only one or two rather deep notes. Four of these are usually used together, playing 'in hocket', each sounding its note at the proper time. The smaller horns are far more flexible, musically speaking. They may have five or six notes and are very resonant. Cow's horns may be used to make hunting horns. Antelope horns are used to make the very piercing and clear-voiced horns used in connection with the agidigbé gong at the secret society dances. I collected the following horn calls at a public ceremony of the Ichahoho Society:

Icáhoho ɔlákɔ́kɔ́ɔ́ɔ́ɔ́ɔ́! 'Ichahoho: fire and pepper!' (The fire-bearer burns pepper up-wind from the spectators).
Icáhoho lɔ́cɛ ŋmó ɛí mǎa pííííí! 'Ichahoho must kill a man this year!'
Ányɔ́pɛ́ otú bǐ, ɔga lɔ́da otúúúúú! 'Bats eat at night; [our] guests eat something at night'' (i.e. they will eat some of the stolen goat).

143

Icáhoho ɛlǎ ka máǎǎǎǎ!? 'Ichahoho, shall the matter drop!?'
Agámá cilɛgba, agámá cilɛgba! (Title of man waving firebrand
of burning grass over spectators).
Ědě ffědě, ědě ffedě! (Akwéya for ɛlɛ ffɛlɛ) 'Madness surpasses
madness!' (i.e.: There is madness and madness.)
Otɔkpa kwɔɔgɔ! 'Spearthrower caught a kite!' (title).
Eléééé lele lé ú! (elééé is the crying over the death of a young
man).

14

Oɲmóolikpó tumɛtumɛ! 'The killer of short-legged ones [goats]'.
Atuma gblɔɔgɔ gblɔɔgɔ! (Title for the Ichahoho Dance).
Icáhoho ɔlá bɔbɔ! 'Ichahoho, the red red fire!'
ijímini kɔmini! 'Secret signs!' (i.e.: 'We speak with secret signs!!'
The words are not analysable in current Idoma).

Since the society horns and the hunting horns have more notes
than they strictly need, they achieve considerable musical expres-
siveness, typically ending with a prolonged note. I first really
knew the extent to which these horn calls are understood when a
young man brought a hunting horn to my house one day. Two of
my neighbours sat with us. He would blow a call, and they would
say the words out without the slightest hesitation. The man with
the horn would smile and nod his assent, while my assistant wrote
the calls down. I collected twenty-six calls in this way in the course
of an hour and a half, and there was never the slightest question
about the interpretations which my neighbours gave to the horn calls.
The Idoma use flutes in great variety. Since they usually have
five or six notes, they 'talk' very clearly and with versatility of
expression. A very common perquisite of a chief is an orchestra
consisting of a big, double-headed bass drum and three flutes.
It is a clear case of lèse majesté for a lesser man to presume to
assemble such an orchestra. Such flutes will call the titles of various
notables present at a gathering, give the various praises of the chief,
and in general offer a running commentary on the proceedings.
The following flute calls are made from a tape recording made at
the royal compound of the Chief of Igumale and are typical:

Otsɛzi ɔgábíidotsɛ iyǐněě sún ɛnwila nɛ, ɛjɛ lotsɛ wɔlǐrɛ́ɲ ee!
'He who sits on the stool, Lion of Lions, King, it is of him I
worry; the leopard with the kingship is no plaything!'
Osi lotsɛ̌ óǒ le ré, ɔwɔ yótsɛ́ nɛ! 'He who is fitting for the kingship,
let him be king; God makes the king!'

Ɔnyɛ zɔ́ɔtŭ oŋmɛ́ɛwɔ́ɔwɔ? 'Who is brave [enough] to kill God's goat?' (i.e., Who is brave enough to harm the king?) otsɛ soláafúŋ́ gotsɛ si lɛ́gɔ́ŋ; otsɛ sotɛ́ɛ̆jĕ lijŏofu. 'The king is not not fit for quarrels and the king is not fit for opponents [ɛ̀gɔ́, literally 'peers, equals']; the king is fit for a dance-compliment of twenty brass rods' (otɛ́ɛ̆jĕ, the placing of a penny on the forehead of a dancer).

aluzií wɔwɔ̆tsɛ ní eee! 'A man's enemies are not his God!'

ɔyólɛ́ɛ̆lă ge kwú, ɔtŭ sɔlazógbɛ́ɛnɛnŭ. 'When the child who seeks trouble dies, his mother's neighbours are pleased.'

ɔ́ɲtsɔ́nyŏoŋmɛ́ɛkwŭ liwĕɪ́ lɛfú, óŏ kwíɪ̆wĕɪ́ ŋmɛ́ɛfú kejĕŋ wɛlɪ̌rɛ́ŋ! 'The girl from the corner with shame on her head, let her take shame from her head, for dancing is no plaything!' ('Come on girls, get out and dance!').

Owɔsĕ wɔ̆gbɔ́ ŕ́mɔ́ogwĕ́ĕjĕ́ĕ̆ yá ńcɛ? 'When the good thing is coming into public, what will the singer do today?' (When a pretty girl comes to dance, how shall the singer prepare for her?)

The flutes are much used, in combination with other instruments, with the 'night masks', which are a fundamental theme of cult in this part of Africa. These are voice disguises and sound makers, rather than body masks. Most of these 'talk', but with a high 'coefficient of weirdness', to use Malinowski's phrase. Other talking instruments which may or may not be used in secret cults (depending on the district) are the seven-string harp, the xylophone, and the small 'piano' mounted in a gourd resonator and played with the thumbs.

Another interesting instrument is a long, narrow gourd, open at both ends. It is illustrated in Meek's *A Sudanese Kingdom*, where a man is shown playing it. In Idoma it is a woman's instrument. The larger end is struck against the thigh, and smaller end being either open or held closed. The hand may strike the smaller end, with the larger end free or held against the thigh. In this way four distinct notes may be obtained. In addition the player strikes the gourd against her seat and slaps her chest. It is an intimate instrument for use in the home, and is often used for telling short stories to children (Jukun 'shintu', Agala Idoma 'ádɔgá').

In Egede and other parts of Idoma Division I found a well-developed yodelling language which can be heard for over a mile. It is used here for 'speaking' according to the principles already set forth here; only the medium is the reinforced falsetto voice characteristic of yodelling. If one comes to visit a friend and finds his compound deserted, it is very polite to announce one's presence in this way. The head of a compound in some districts will use it every morning in a formal greeting to the heads of the families under him. He enquires as to their health and plans for the day. The relation of the dance in Africa to the talking instruments which often guide it is worth our attention. When a dancer follows with his body the rhythms of a talking instrument which he understands, he may be said to be talking with his body. This fact has only occurred to me since leaving the field, so I cannot say that I have studied the phenomenon. I have discussed it with various West Africans, however, and find that they readily admit to knowledge of the 'talking dance'. It remains to be seen whether this dance-speech is a purely passive thing, a full-body response to something heard, or whether the audience can understand a message merely by watching a skillful dancer, in the absence of drums and other musical instruments. In either case, it is evident that the intimate union of speech, music and dance surrounds the West African with an exceedingly rich, artistic medium of communication. When one watches infants being carried into the dance on their mothers' back, one knows that what they learn in this way is deeply learned.

Talking musical instruments can be most useful as pedagogical devices to help Africans learn to write their own languages. In my experience, Africans have great difficulty learning to write the tones consistently. They constantly get highs and lows mixed, etc. I thought for a time that this is due to the fact that (contrary to what Carrington and Rattay report for the Congo and the Gold Coast) the normal terminology for tone in Idoma and neighbouring regions reverses what a European would expect; for the high tone is the male tone and the low is the female tone. (The high tone is said to be the stronger, and hence male). I wondered, as does Carrington, whether we are not unnaturally forcing a European metaphor which equates geometrical 'upness' and 'downness' with greater wave frequency and its opposite. I concluded, however, that this cannot be the explanation, for I found that illiterate drummers also speak quite literally of tone which 'go up' (ɔkogicŏ) and tones which 'go down' (ɔkogɛháajɛ), meaning by them the same tones we mean, viz.: male and female, respectively (in their terminology). My best explanation at the moment goes back to what I said at the beginning of this paper, namely, that the tone of a syllable uttered in isolation is in principle not identifiable. To this one must add the confusing fact that the junctures between the constituent words of a compound word are phonetically tighter than the junctures of the syllables of a simple word. This makes it extremely difficult for the native-speakers to identify word boundaries (for which clearcut morphological criteria exist, however). There is the further fact that the native speaker seldom thinks of the words in isolation, but rather in their contexts, where their tones vary. Whatever the reason, it is my experience that Africans must undergo quite a lot of drill, beginning with simple paradigms, before they can write consistently. In this the slit-log gongs are most useful. The student is made to 'say' the word or phrase on the gong, and then there is no arguing with what he has just done with his hands. It seems to me, too, that the use of drums in class would lend interest to primary instruction, even though it might disturb the neighbours!

Rattray has described the organization of many drums into a communications net in Ashanti. Such a system requires a considerable concentration of political power in a central government. I have seen nothing resembling a communications net in Idoma. The big slit-log gongs can be heard for from five to ten miles during the quiet time of day. This is sufficient for most purposes, since the separate and independent Lands seldom had a radius of more than ten miles. The Tiv make quite tremendous gongs (indyer). I have seen some which are nine feet long and three to four feet in diameter. I was told that they can be heard for twenty miles and that Tiv country has a whole informal communications net composed of them (I was unable to check this statement). The big drums are an important instrument of propaganda in time of war. The Bohannans, who experienced a war between the Tiv and the Bete, of Obudu Division, have told me that the psychological impact is tremendous when a great drum says 'War! War! War!' for two or three days without stopping.

Drumming is a highly skilled, if part-time, profession, and goes in certain families. One only has to try it to realize that great discipline of muscular control is necessary. I have already mentioned the reluctance of the drummers to talk about their methods and the fact that young, aspiring drummers must watch for opportunities to practise on the important drums. The drummers must be paid for their services, and often feel that their importance to the community is not properly appreciated. They are quite capable of holding up a big dance while they bargain. An Idoma friend tells me, 'When an African hears his name drummed, he must jump up for joy even from his sick bed.' He will dance before the drums and then greet them with pennies or shillings, depending on his position in the feast or the play taking place. One's drum name is quite elaborate and is usually compounded of references to one's father's lineage, to events in one's personal life, and to one's personal name.

It remains to be said that among large groups in the towns and among the educated Nigerians, the art of drum talk is dying out rapidly. I found that near the Divisional Headquarters town of Oturkpo, drummer boys did not know how to make the common type of membrane drum talk, and were just pounding it without meaning. The elders backed me up when I explained the method. The school teachers and students think much more of the glamorous European snare drums, and it is these which they acquire. Another phase of the problem is that the drummers play a key role in the old social structure, and they do not collaborate easily with the schools. It would take not only a strong desire but also a lot of patience and tact to arrive at a good working arrangement between the drummers and the local school. This is not to say that the art is dying out in an absolute sense. The population of Nigeria is increasing rapidly, and it may well be that one may find a large 'detribalized' or 'decultured' town and city population and simultaneously an absolute increase in the countryside of the numbers of people who actually operate institutions which we consider old and indigenous. Apart from this, one sees and hears plenty of talking drums in the big cities, like Ibadan and Lagos. It must be said too that the Nigerian nationalists are beginning to take an interest in such African arts as the dance. Should this trend continue, I do not think that they will neglect the talking drums.

Robert G. Armstrong

Joan Rayfield and her husband spent the past eight years in isolated mining camps in Uganda, Western Australia, and Queensland. She is now a graduate student in anthropology at the University of Toronto.

Jorge Luis Borges, poet and lecturer, was educated in Geneva and Madrid, and then returned to Argentina where, with Ricardo Guiraldes, he founded the journal *Proa* and translated Gide, Kafka, Faulkner, and Virginia Woolf.

Anthony Kerrigan, whose beautiful translation of *Hojoki*, done with Thomas Rowe, appeared in *Explorations 3*, also translated *Mutations*. He is now the Art Editor of the *American Peoples Encyclopedia*.

E. E. Cummings' poem is reprinted from *Poems 1923–1954*, Harcourt, Brace and Company, copyright, 1926, 1954.

Dorothy Lee's paper was read before the Culture and Communication Seminar at the University of Louisville.

Rev. Walter Ong, S. J., is on the staff of the English Department, St. Louis University. His article was written while he was a Guggenheim Fellow.

Stephen Gilman, Professor of Spanish, Harvard University, is lecturing this year at Bonn as a Ford Foundation Fellow.

Lawrence Frank, 72 Perry Street, New York, is the author of *Society as the Patient* and other works. His paper is a precis, which he allowed the editor to make, of a detailed monograph on tactilism, part of which was delivered at the Culture and Communication Seminar held at the University of Louisville in the Fall of 1954.

Millar MacLure is Assistant Professor of English, Victoria College.

Marjorie Adix's account of a conference held by Dylan Thomas with students at the University of Utah is reprinted from *Encounter.*

Robert Armstrong, 2820 Jessup Road, Cincinnati, Ohio, studied at Oxford and Chicago, where he took his doctorate in anthropology, and then spent two years in Nigeria. At present he is in business with his father.

Recently we obtained a number of directives circulated inside various mass-media organizations and decided to reprint two. The television one is given in full, but the memo from *Time, Inc.* has been cut in half. We did not have room for one written by a well-known psychoanalyst for a home permanent company and sent to their ad writers. It explained why a neutralizer should be sold with each home permanent kit. Tight curls, it said, are symbolic of pubic hair and might prove embarrassing if a woman weren't prepared to see the thing through. Last week we saw one of this company's ads, and there it was, rephrased and hidden, but the same message.